INTERNATIONAL SERIES OF
MONOGRAPHS ON COMPUTER SCIENCE

General Editors

THE INTERNATIONAL SERIES OF
MONOGRAPHS ON COMPUTER SCIENCE

Derivation and Validation of Software Metrics

MARTIN SHEPPERD

Department of Computing and Cognition
Bournemouth University

and

DARREL INCE

Department of Computing
The Open University

CLARENDON PRESS · OXFORD
1993

Oxford University Press, Walton Street, Oxford OX2 6DP

Oxford New York Toronto
Delhi Bombay Calcutta Madras Karachi
Kuala Lumpur Singapore Hong Kong Tokyo
Nairobi Dar es Salaam Cape Town
Melbourne Auckland Madrid
and associated companies in
Berlin Ibadan

Oxford is a trade mark of Oxford University Press

Published in the United States by
Oxford University Press Inc., New York

A catalogue record for this book is available from the British Library

Library of Congress Cataloging in Publication Data
(Available on request)

ISBN 0–19–853842–1

Typeset by Darrel Ince
Printed in Great Britain by Biddles Ltd., Guildford & King's Lynn

PREFACE

The last twenty years has witnessed an increasing trend — seen in both academia and industry — of regarding software development as an engineering discipline. One area which characterizes a mature engineering discipline is that of measurement; for example, production engineers are now able to predict accurately the number of reject ball-bearings that are produced in a factory from a consideration of the performance of the machine-tools that are used to produce those ball-bearings.

The area of software measurement — more commonly known as software metrics — is one where researchers have been very active for about 25 years, and it represents one of the clearest attempts to transform software development into engineering. Workers in this area have been attempting to answer hard questions such as:

- Is it possible to predict the error-proneness of a system using measurements taken from its system design?

- Is it possible to extract quantitative features from the representation of a software design to enable us to predict the degree of maintainability of a software system?

- Are there any quantifiable, key features of the program code of a module* that would enable us to predict the degree of difficulty of testing for that module, and the number of residual errors in the module after a particular level of testing has occurred.

- Is it possible to extract quantifiable features from the representation of a software design to enable us to predict the amount of effort required to build the software described by that design?

- Are there quantifiable features that can be extracted from the program code of a subroutine that can be used to help predict the amount of effort required to test the subroutine?

Given the amount of resource put into metrics research over the last few decades it is, perhaps, surprising that progress has been slow. This is, in some degree, due to the complex nature of software development, but it is also due to some methodological problems. It is these problems that this book is intended to address.

---

*Whenever the term *module* occurs in this book we mean a chunk of code which can be called from a point in a program which, after it has been called, returns to the statement after the call. Examples include the function in C, the procedure in Pascal and the subroutine in COBOL

In brief, our thesis is that researchers have not addressed the modelling aspects of software metrication sufficiently, and this has resulted in ill-defined metrics, poor empirical validations, and a concern with metaphysics which is wholly at variance with the need for the precisely defined measures that our software projects cry out for.

We hope that two classes of readers will be able to access this book. First, researchers in software engineering will find a discussion of the role of measurement on software projects, and a methodology which is able to guide them during the tricky process of defining and validating software metrics. The second audience is that of staff working in the software industry. In particular, we hope that they will find the first three review chapters a useful starting point in their study of software metrics. We hope these chapters will help them to guard against precipitate decisions in implementing a software metrication programme.

Finally, we would both like to thank Sheila Shepherd for the copy-editing that she carried out on this book, it improved it immensely; we would also like to acknowledge Professor Manny Lehman for providing a large number of perceptive comments on an early draft.

Bournemouth   M.S.
Milton Keynes   D.I.
April 1993

CONTENTS

1

INTRODUCTION

Synopsis

This chapter outlines the problem area which the material in this
book addresses, namely, the application of quantitative methods
— popularly known as software metrics — to software engineering
and the design of system architectures or structures in particular.
It is argued that this is of considerable significance because of the
potential impact of poor design decisions upon a wide range of
quality factors of a system when it is finally implemented. The
software engineering background to the book is then described.
The chapter concludes with an outline of the structure of the book
and a summary of its key points.

1.1   The problem area

This book is concerned with quantitative approaches to software engineering, otherwise known as software metrics. Within this rather broad domain
the book addresses a particular concern: the production of software system designs. To date, the main thrust of research in software metrics has
been towards the measurement of code, yet it is our belief that by the time
the code is available for measurement, the majority of a software project's
resources have been committed, so that any strategic changes in direction become prohibitively expensive. Therefore, the emphasis of this book
will be upon metrics that can be extracted, and acted upon, during the
earlier stages of a software project. Since software engineering was first
proposed as a discipline in its own right in 1968,[144] the primary focus of attention has moved progressively earlier and earlier in the so-called project
life-cycle. For much of the 1960s and 1970s the major debates concerned
code and how to structure the control flow, as exemplified in the work of
Dijkstra,[48] Dahl *et al.*,[44] and Wirth.[212] However, more recently, interest
has begun to focus upon the design aspects of software, evidenced by the
work of Parnas,[152, 153] which addresses the criteria for the modularization
of software and its impact upon the maintenance characteristics of systems.
Another example is Jackson's well-known boating lake case study,[97] which
demonstrated the impact of design decisions upon the maintainability of
the resultant code. The conclusion reached in this particular work was that

although structured programming techniques were important, they could not compensate for deficiencies in the design.

More recently still, attention has turned to those stages of a project which precede design. These activities are grouped together under the term *requirements engineering*, the aim of which is to transform and tailor the informal system requirements of the user or customer into a more structured specification document, which is then used by the software developers. Clearly, if this document does not describe the required system accurately and unambiguously, then no design methodology and no amount of structured programming will prevent the system being developed from failing to satisfy the user, with consequent costly rewrites. These rewrites are especially expensive since they imply the maximum amount of backtracking because specification, design, and coding must redone. Acknowledgement of the significance of these potential problems has led to the proliferation of structured systems analysis methods,[6, 26, 46] and also to an upsurge of interest in the application of mathematics to the creation and validation of specifications.[101, 138, 205] It is evident, then, that the early stages of the software development process, such as requirements analysis and design, are critical to the successful implementation of software systems. It is now widely recognized that errors committed and poor decisions made during these early stages result in the most costly and intractable problems.[24] Unfortunately, feedback concerning such problems is usually not available until late in the development process — often during integration testing or even later.

As has already been stated the major concern of this book is with system design: the process of developing an overall system structure. We have concentrated on this activity because of its impact upon such system quality factors as maintainability and implementation effort. In other words, for a given specification — namely the one that the user or customer wants — there are a variety of designs or outline solutions. These various solutions cannot be considered to be equivalent in terms of their impact upon system quality factors, despite the fact that they all implement the same set of requirements.

Decisions made during design concerning system architecture have a special significance for the maintainability, reliability, and ease of implementation of the resultant software. Given the absence of immediate feedback, the designer is forced to make *ad hoc* decisions concerning alternative architectures, with little understanding of their consequences in terms of impact upon the characteristics of the system being developed.

Design methodologies such as Structured Design,[195] Jackson Structured Programming,[97] and Object Oriented Design,[25] attempt to address the problem of very late feedback by providing guide-lines for the generation of system structures and design evaluation criteria. The benefits of such methodologies are considerable; however, *they are not mechanistic and the evaluation criteria tend to be qualitative and subjective*, as evidenced by the terms *module coupling* and *module cohesion*.[142]

Although the bulk of metrics research has addressed program code, various design-based metrics have been proposed to address the shortcomings of current approaches to software design. In particular, there has been a search for measures that can predict such quality factors as maintainability while the software development is still at the design stage. Another objective of researchers has been to provide objective, quantitative evaluation criteria that can be used to compare competing system architectures. Though design metrics are potentially very important for the software engineer, there has been limited work on their validation;* consequently, many of the findings have been contradictory.† This, we suspect, is one of the main reasons why there has been little or almost no take-up of metrics by the software industry.

The dichotomy between the importance of applying quantitative methods to the design of system architecture, and the absence of consistent results, or widely accepted metrics, typifies the area of software measurement at present. We feel that if software engineering is truly to become an engineering discipline, then quantitative models and the use of measurement are imperative. Yet, at present, there appears to be little progress in this direction. This is a theme that this book will return to on more than one occasion.

1.2 The book

As has already been stated, there is a need to develop metrics that provide useful quantitative feedback for staff involved in developing of software system designs. This feedback would enable the designer to understand the consequences of a particular design decision better, to compare candidate structures, to be able to identify critical parts of an architecture as potential maintenance 'hot spots', and to guide design inspections to focus on the most troublesome areas.‡

However, this first aim leads to a number of further supporting aims. The adjective *useful* has been emphasized in the foregoing discussion. This introduces the need for validation. There is no shortage of metrics;[41] what

---

*There are, of course, exceptions and we would cite the work reported in Card and Agresti[31] and Troy and Zweben[204] as examples of thoughtful and useful studies.

†An example of contradictory findings concerns the design metric of Henry and Kafura[82] known as *information flow*. Although Henry and Kafura report strong empirical support from their study of the UNIX operating system, other studies have been far more equivocal, for instance the study of the VME operating system by Kitchenham.[112] Unfortunately, at present, no adequate framework exists for comparing these studies or reconciling differing claims

‡These ideas are further developed in Shepperd and Ince,[184] in particular it is shown how design metrics may be employed to refine a system architecture successively.

is less in evidence, though, are metrics that are generally valid, usable, and useful, and thus widely accepted.

The problem of conflicting empirical evidence has already been touched upon. This suggests that although the first concern of this research is with system architecture metrics, it will be necessary to evolve a general framework for the development of software metrics, evaluation, and application. In a sense, this must be a research objective which bridges the gap that Belady identifies between the 'speculators' and the 'doers'.[20]

It is also important to identify, from the outset, areas that will not be addressed by the research described in this book. Frequently, metrics are characterized as either product or process metrics.[178] As their name implies, the former are measurements derived from software engineering products, for example software designs, test suites, and code, and the latter are measurements that are extracted from software engineering processes, such as the number of faults uncovered in a design inspection. Although these two classes of metrics are related, this research will not deal explicitly with process measurements.

1.3 Some definitions

Before we proceed further it is probably appropriate to consider some definitions. First, the term *metric*. Unfortunately, there is no generally agreed definition. Some workers use the term interchangeably with 'measurement'. Others distinguish between measurement and metric, where metric indicates a measurement and an underlying model or theory. The latter is intended to emphasize the need for measurement to be placed into the context of a theory. Although laudable in its aim there is such a divergence between it and reality — as will be shown in subsequent chapters — that we do not believe such a definition to be very helpful. Accordingly, within this book a metric merely conveys a measurement of a software engineering product or process — no more and no less. Although we are unhappy with this weak meaning, it provides a useful starting point for the book.

It might also be useful to consider what is meant by *design*. In a very abstract sense, design encompasses any activity where there is an element of choice or decision making. Without choice the activity is entirely deterministic and hence may be fully automated. It is customary within software engineering to distinguish between *high-level design* and *detailed design*. The former is concerned with architecture — for example the choice of modules, their interfaces, and data structures — while the latter is concerned with matters closer to implementation, such as the specification of algorithms.* This book is concerned with the former because it is available

---

*It is worth pointing out that there is no uniform terminology. For example, some software developers combine what we describe as system design and detailed design into one process which they refer to as design.

earlier in the software life-cycle, and because it is believed to have a greater impact upon implementation effort, reliability, and maintainability.[194, 220] One major restriction is imposed: the research described here will focus upon the design of 'function strong' systems (for instance, a reactor control system), as opposed to 'data strong' systems (for instance, a library catalogue system).[47] Again, the reason for this is primarily a pragmatic one so as to restrict the area of research.*

1.4 The organization of the book

The book is organized into three sections.

- We review existing software metrics and metrics research. Although we have a particular interest in design metrics, all metrics derived from any software engineered product will be scrutinized in a search for any underlying trends or general patterns.
- We describe a general framework for the development or selection of software metrics, followed by evaluation and application. In inventing such a framework it may be necessary to borrow from other disciplines such as classical measurement theory, experimental design, and statistics.
- We outline the development and evaluation of a measure, or set of measures, using the framework described above, in order to meet the original goal of helping the software designer to choose between alternative system architectures in order to improve the ease of implementation, the reliability of implementation, and the ease of maintenance. It is expected that applying the method to an actual measurement problem — that of developing design metrics — will yield information concerning the utility of the method itself.

The research described here will be of little value if all that emerges is yet more untested and unvalidated metrics. There is certainly no shortage, at present, of such metrics.[42, 178] Instead the themes of method and evaluation will recur throughout the text.

Chapter 2 reviews the current state of metrics research with respect to specification, design, and code metrics. We pay particular attention to the evaluation of the various metrics described. Chapter 3 offers a detailed dissection of three of the most popular and influential metrics, where it is argued that all suffer from a similar malaise: weak underlying models and unconvincing empirical validations. Chapter 4 examines two past attempts to overcome the malaise of weak modelling. Chapter 5 provides

---

*Subsequent to the research described here, we have commenced an investigation into the possibility of providing data designers with quantitative feedback. Early results, described in Ince and Shepperd,[92, 93] suggest that at least some of principles for functional design are appropriate for data modelling.

a simple tutorial which describes our attempt to bring modelling notions
to the fore in the development of metrics. Chapters 6 and 7 show the
gradual development of what we believe is a useful metric for measuring
design complexity. Chapter 8 summarizes some of the achievements of the
work reported here and points out further work which could be carried out
using the material described in this book. The aim of these chapters is
to show how our ideas concerning modelling can be employed to derive an
industrially useful design metric. It is worth stressing that these chapters
are not an attempt to sell one metric, but, rather, an attempt to show a
realistic development of a metric — including the inevitable false trails,
compromises, and backtracking that modelling inevitably produces. The
final chapter is a summary of the book. The main points that we stress
throughout the book are:

- One must be concerned with the context of a metric as well as the
  metric itself in order to have meaningful measurement.
- Measurable software products are not restricted to code. There are
  many important benefits to be realized from metrics derived early on
  in the software life-cycle.
- It is insufficient to propose metrics without supporting empirical investigation — preferably from a variety of environments. The domain
  of relevance and degree of significance of any metrics must be established and demonstrated by validation.
- Metrics must reflect some phenomenology and their validation and
  extension requires models of the phenomenology.

2

SOFTWARE METRICS REVIEWED

Synopsis

This chapter reviews developments in the field of software metrics from the early 1970s to the present time. Metrics can be categorized according to the stage of software development with which they are associated. Thus we have code metrics, design metrics, and specification metrics. Although our primary interest in this book is with software designs, code measures will also be examined. The chapter indicates briefly that the area of software metrics is afflicted by a number of serious problems, a theme expanded upon in the following chapter.

2.1 Introduction

This chapter is a brief review of work carried out in the metrics area over the last three decades. In a number of ways both this chapter and Chapter 3, which describes three metrics in detail, present a rather bleak view of what is a potentially promising and important field of software engineering. There are several recurring themes in both the chapters.

First, the majority of metrics are presented in such a fashion that it is unclear exactly what is being measured. Terms such as 'complexity' and 'quality' proliferate. As a direct result, empirical evaluations have interpreted metrics in widely differing ways. Divergent results have ensued for every metric evaluated above. Almost the only unifying feature has been the strong statistical associations with size metrics such as lines of code.*

Second the metrics appear to be based upon very ambitious models of software, in that their proponents anticipated that one or two (at the most) measures would be able to predict a wide range of software quality factors in an equally wide range of applications and environments.

Third, the majority of early life-cycle metrics have been subjected to minimal levels of empirical analysis. The most notable exception is the information flow metric;[82] however, even in this instance, the results have an air of ambivalence about them.

---

*A rather awkward result which has been ignored by the research community.

Fourth, although useful applications exist for code metrics, there is little doubt that design and specification metrics are the way to proceed. There are three reasons for this:

- They provide much earlier feedback about the nature of the software product.

- They measure aspects of software that are more abstract than program code, namely function and structure — the difficulty with code metrics being that they tend to be oriented towards specific languages or types of applications.

- Most design metrics — especially those based on measures that include inter-modular aspects of complexity — are founded on much more convincing models of software complexity than those models that are based on counting aspects of program code, certainly models that are more in line with current thinking in software engineering.

2.2   Metrics: a brief history

In the early 1950s and 1960s problems of computer hardware resources tended to be the most pressing. As a result, measurement was almost universally targeted at the issues of computational time and the memory requirements of algorithms. However, this is no longer the case. From the 1970s onwards, developments in computer hardware have outstripped progress in software technology. Most costs and bottle-necks are now associated with the software parts of a computer system.[24] This has been matched by a parallel movement in software metrics which is now directed at measuring properties of software systems that lead to the consumption of human resources (e.g. programming effort, reliability, etc.) rather than hardware resources, since these tend to be less costly.

This interest in human resources expended on the development and operation of software systems has manifested itself as an attempt to quantify software complexity. Complexity is perceived as the 'root of all evil'* and if only it could be reduced this would bring about attendant reductions in all manner of software evils such as: excessive development and testing effort, unreliability, and unmaintainability. Despite the obvious appeal of such a proposition, software complexity has proved to be a rather intractable problem — notwithstanding the large amount of attention that has been focused in its direction.

From the early 1970s onwards, software engineers have attempted to measure software complexity by concentrating mainly upon a few syntactical properties of program code, for example the number of tokens or the number of program decisions. Towards the end of the 1970s a growing realization occurred that many of the most costly and least desirable

---

*To paraphrase St Paul more accurately, 'love of complexity is the root of all evil' (1 Timothy ch. 6 v 10)!

software attributes were the consequence of problems during the design stage.[46, 97, 152, 194] It was thus a natural progression to consider measuring properties of designs in order to identify complexity earlier in the software life-cycle. This has proved less straightforward than one might imagine for a number of reasons. First, there has been a lack of standardization in the practice of design and even in the use of design notation. Second, no researchers have yet been able to give an adequate definition of the term *complexity*. Nevertheless, a number of design metrics have been proposed.

Given the trend in increasing concern for the early stages of the software life-cycle, it is hardly surprising that in the 1980s and 1990s there have been some attempts to measure specifications, although these have been targeted at project size and effort estimation rather than at complexity as such. The main problem here is that specifications tend to be even less standardized or structured than designs, leading to problems of comparability of measurements. Even so, the management benefits of obtaining early predictions of system development effort and cost are such that there have been an increasing number of metrics developed in this area over the last decade.

The remainder of this chapter, surveys what may loosely be called software complexity metrics,* commencing with code metrics and then progressing back through the software life-cycle.

2.3   Code metrics

2.3.1   *Lines of code*

The simplest software complexity metric is lines of code (LOC). The basis for LOC is that program length can be used as a predictor of such program characteristics as reliability and ease of maintenance. Despite, or possibly even because of, the simplicity of this metric, it has been almost universally reviled,[47, 52, 133] the main reason being that it can easily be changed and manipulated by the programmer, and it is often just a matter of style how a programmer arranges program code in a listing. Certainly there are serious difficulties with defining what actually constitutes a line of code; consequently modifications such as the number of source statements or machine code instructions generated have been advanced. None of these modifications could exactly be described as being in vogue with the metrics community.

The suggestion by Basili and Hutchens[11] that the LOC metric be regarded as a baseline metric to which all other metrics be compared is

---

*We will return to the matter of software complexity at a later stage and argue that it is undefined to the extent that it defies measurement; consequently, it is the source of the fruitlessness of much current work and, hence, should be dropped as a measurement objective. Nevertheless, we will use conventional nomenclature in the meantime, in order to minimize confusion.

appropriate. It would be reasonable to expect an effective code metric to perform better than LOC and so, as a minimum, LOC offers a 'null hypothesis' for empirical evaluations of software metrics.*

2.3.2 Software Science metrics

An early attempt to provide a code metric based on a model of software complexity was provided by the late Maurice Halstead was based on a wide variety of sources: from thermodynamics, information theory, and cognitive psychology to reverse compilation.[74] The eventual result was a set of general laws that Halstead postulated as being analogous to natural laws.[74, 75] Halstead's original focus was algorithms, but it soon widened to: 'linguistics, psychology, or any field dealing with Man the Symbol Manipulator',[74] and even to such fields as developmental psychology and the analysis of literary texts.[76] In the following chapter we demonstrate major weaknesses with this metric.

2.3.3 Graph theoretic measures

An alternative but equally influential code metric is McCabe's cyclomatic complexity.[133] In developing this metric McCabe had two objectives: first, to predict the effort of testing the software, and thereby identify appropriate decompositions of the software into modules; second, to predict complexity-related characteristics of the resultant software.

Given the increasing costs of software development, McCabe stated[133] that what was required was a:

> mathematical technique that will provide a quantitative basis for
> modularisation and allow us to identify software modules that
> will be difficult to test or maintain.

Lines of code (LOC) metric was deemed to be an inadequate approach: McCabe could see no relationship between length and module complexity. Instead, he posited that the number of control paths through a module would be a better indicator, especially since it had a strong relationship with testing effort. Furthermore, much of the work on 'structured programming' in the early 1970s emphazised program control flow structures.[44]

The model that McCabe adopted was to view software as a directed graph, with edges representing the flow of control and nodes as statements. In effect this is a simplified flow chart. Complexity was seen as being related to control flow complexity: the more loops, jumps, and selections a program contains, the more complex it is to understand. Assuming that psychological or cognitive complexity is the target of the measurement process, several modifications have been proposed that take into account the

---

*In passing it is also worth noting that much empirical work[12, 82, 109] has shown the metric to correlate strongly with other metrics, most notably McCabe's cyclomatic complexity,[133] as demonstrated by Shepperd.[176]

structuredness of the software. The proponents of these modifications argue
that to consider each decision in isolation is an inidcation of an inadequate
model of program complexity, and that the 'cognitive load' is a product
of the way in which decisions are combined. In other words, a contextual
view is required. Thus, one development of McCabe's metric has been to
incorporate a notion of nesting depth.[51, 79, 132, 156, 158]

Other researchers have modified the cyclomatic complexity metric in
order to capture the degree to which the control flow of a piece of software is structured, in the sense described by Dijkstra[48] and Dahl et al.,[44]
among others. Woodward et al.[216] present their knot metric, which uses
the number of arc intersections of a program flow graph as an index of
structuredness. A fully structured program will have zero knots. The authors report that in a library of FORTRAN sub-routines, approximately
one-third had zero knots, one-third had less than 10 knots, and less than
one-sixth over 20 knots. Brown and Fischer[29] describe a software tool to
automate the analysis of program flow graphs in order to identify non-
structured control flow constructs. These ideas tend, however, to make the
implicit assumption that the target program is at least FORTRAN-esque
and so they have limited applicability.

Control flow complexity has continued to exercise the minds and imaginations of many metrics researchers. Zolnowski[221] has reported that in
his study of software complexity factors, software developers indicated that
eight out of nine control flow measures were rated as very important. It is,
therefore, hardly surprising that suggestions for control flow measures, most
derived from McCabe's original work, continued apace. Schneiderman and
Hoffman[160] have defined control flow metrics based on the minimum number of paths and node reachability.* They reported significant correlations
between these measures against the number of errors and the time taken
to find errors. Furthermore, they noted that these metrics out-performed
both McCabe's metric and LOC. Subsequent variations on this theme include Iyengar et al.,[96] Negrini and Sami,[146] Sinha et al.,[188] and Stetter[191].
However, no empirical validations are offered. More novel is the attempt
by Hall and Preiser[73] to apply cyclomatic complexity to software designs.
Again, no empirical support is provided. Possibly the most imaginative
of all is the suggestion by Samson et al.[167] that the number of axioms in
an algebraic specification† will be equivalent to the $v(G)$ of the resulting
implementation. We will return to this last suggestion when reviewing
specification metrics.

A contrasting approach to program control complexity is due to Chen.[35]

---

*These metrics are only feasible with the restriction that paths traversing a backward
branch more than once are excluded.

†An algebraic specification consists of a series of mathematical axioms which describe
the behaviour of a system.

An information theoretic viewpoint is adopted whereby the source comprises only two distinct characters, a sequence and a selection, but may be infinitely long, thus most* program structures may be described. The entropy of a source is used to capture the relationship between control flow complexity and programmer productivity. Chen presents results that are suggestive of some empirical relationship, although he hypothesizes that may be quantized rather than continuous. Davis and LeBlanc describe similar work.[45]

To summarize, there has been — and still is — much interest in capturing software complexity in terms of the complexity of control flow. There have been various approaches to measuring control flow complexity. These range from McCabe's simple model,[133] which can be characterized by the number of simple decisions plus one, to more sophisticated models that account for nesting depth, such as Piowarski,[156] or are based upon considerations of entropy.[35] Of these metrics, cyclomatic complexity is the most thoroughly studied, with studies to correlate the metric with error-proneness, maintainability, understandability, and development effort producing erratic results. The most startling observations are the consistently high correlations with LOC and the out-performing of $v(G)$ by LOC in a significant number of cases.[11, 42, 109, 151, 208] Few of the other metrics described have been subjected to anything other than the most cursory empirical scrutiny, a point emphasized by a review of graph-theoretic metrics in Shepperd.[176]

More serious still is the confusion concerning what is being measured. In his original paper McCabe[133] seemed to alternate between the idea of measuring testing difficulty, providing guide-lines for the modularization of software, and capturing the cognitive or psychological complexity of the software. A subsequent report[134] concentrated on developing 'programs that are not inherently untestable'. McCabe's underlying model is examined in more detail in the following chapter.

2.3.4   *Hybrid metrics*

As a consequence of the shortcomings of the more straightforward code-based product metrics, attention has been given to combining the best aspects of existing metrics. Such metrics are frequently termed *hybrid metrics*.

Harrison and Magel[79] have attempted to combine Halstead's metric with a modification of McCabe's metric based on nesting level. They argue that neither metric is sufficient individually. However, when used in combination, a metric results that is 'more intuitively satisfying'. No further validation is offered.

---

*We say *most* advisedly since one might anticipate certain difficulties with exception handling in a language such as Ada.

A similar approach was adopted by Oviedo,[150] who combined control flow and data flow into a single program complexity metric. The metric was validated by applying it to a number of 'good' and 'bad' programs published in the literature. Although a start, this hardly represents a serious effort at empirical validation.

Hansen[78] has proposed a pair of cyclomatic complexity and operand count (defined to be arithmetical operators, function and sub-routine calls, assignments, input and output statements, and array subscription). However, the value of pairs as useful metrics has been strongly questioned.[9, 39] This is because comparisons are difficult to make between differing measurements, for example $\langle a,b \rangle$ and $\langle c,d \rangle$ where $a < c$ and $b > d$. More formally, we do not have a closure of the $>$ relation, and thus we cannot generate even a weak order. These problems are addressed in the section describing classical measurement theory in Chapter 4.

Potier et al.[157] describe an intriguing method of bypassing the problem of n-tuples by constructing a decision tree. In their study of error data, both Software Science and cyclomatic measures are combined, the aim being to identify error-prone modules. Using non-parametric discriminant analysis, various threshold values were identified for the different metrics that were then entered into a decision tree. Curiously, program vocabulary, n, was found to be the metric most effective at discriminating between reliable and error-prone modules, and was thus placed at the top of the tree. It was not reported whether LOC was examined as a potential discriminant, although, given the widely discovered association between LOC and the Software Science measures, one might suspect that it would perform well. This also highlights a problem of using statistically driven metrics in that extremely bizarre models may emerge — as in this case where it is difficult to see the impact of n upon the number of errors other than as a proxy for module size. Even when using decision trees to combine metrics into a composite, one metric tends to predominate, namely the one applied at the root node of the decision tree. Consequently, the approach may not always be applicable.

Arguably, the most extreme variant of the hybrid approach is the one put forward by Munson and Koshgoftaar[140, 141] in the form of their relative complexity metric. They state that:

> ...unlike other metrics, the relative complexity metric combines, simultaneously, all attribute dimensions of *all* complexity metrics.*

The approach is entirely statistical in that it is based upon the factor analysis of an arbitrary set of code metrics, without regard for the meaning of the base set metrics. Consequently, as the authors state, there is no limit

---

*The emphasis is ours.

to the number of metrics that might be combined. What the resultant relative complexity metric means is a quite different proposition.

Despite the very real difficulties of integrating metrics, Kafura and Canning[102] have argued that:

> The interplay between and among the resources and factors is
> too subtle and fluid to be observed accurately by a single metric
> or a single resource.

Basili and Rombach put forward a similar argument[16] in that a single metric is seldom adequate to capture software properties of interest. This creates something of a dilemma. The vector approach to software measurement leads, at best, to semi-orders. The reason why measurement vectors do not permit the generation of at least weak orders is that there is no underlying model with which to link the individual vector elements. The relationship between measurement and metric is explored in Chapter 4.

On the other hand, single metrics in isolation are too simplistic to provide adequate explanations for software engineering phenomena. This would seem to suggest that either metrics and models should be restricted to simpler areas and facets of software engineering, or we must start to regard software more as a system, by which many factors and resources are integrated. Should the latter be accomplished this would provide the basis for at least weak ordering.

2.3.5   Code metrics summary

In short, despite attracting a considerable level of attention in the research community, none of the code metrics described above can be regarded as particularly promising. The recurring pattern is one of researchers correlating metrics (applying different counting rules) to differing software quality factors and obtaining divergent results. Strong associations with program-size measures appear to be the only invariant results. Some metrics might be useful when tailored to specific environments and problems, but as a general means of obtaining insights into, and as a means of combating, software complexity, they have little to commend them. An important reason for this state of affairs is the highly simplistic uni-dimensional models of single resources that underlie the metrics described so far. This, coupled with the fact that code metrics are only available late in a project, and give the developer limited scope for acting on any information provided by the metric, suggests that attention is better directed towards design and specification measures.

2.4   Design metrics

Unlike code metrics, design metrics can be obtained at a much earlier stage in the software development process. They have the advantage that, if necessary, the design can be reworked in order to avoid anticipated problems with the final product well before program code has been produced. Early feedback has been the main motivation for work in the field of design metrics.

Most interest has centred around structural or architectural aspects of a design, sometimes termed *high-level design*. The architecture describes the way in which the system is divided into components, and how the components are interrelated. Some measures also require information extracted from low-level design (i.e. the internal logic of design components, often expressed in a program design language). It is perhaps surprising that there has been little consideration of database systems where there is little functionality, and most of the design effort is directed towards the data model. An exception is deMarco's 'Bang' metric,[47] which is derived from entity relationship diagrams. This is described more fully in a later section.

There are two general problems that all design metrics encounter: the lack of sufficiently formal notations, and validation difficulties. Ideally, a metric should be extracted automatically; certainly, all the relevant information must be available. However, software engineers tend to use a wide variety of notations, many of them informal, for instance by placing excessive reliance upon natural language descriptions. This makes it very difficult to extract meaningful measurements. To counter this, a number of special purpose notations have been proposed[18, 28, 88] or conformance to suitable existing notations such as module hierarchy charts.[22, 34, 219, 36] Another alternative has been to infer design or structural properties from the resultant code.[82] Such an approach must be considered a last resort since the advantages of early feedback are squandered.

Validation difficulties, in particular separating characteristics arising via the design from characteristics induced at a later stage, such as coding errors and poor testing, are in part responsible for the paucity of empirical validations of design metrics. It is, perhaps, unfortunate, as Belady[20] remarks, that there exist two sub-cultures within the software engineering community: the 'speculators' and the 'doers'. As far as design metrics are concerned, the 'speculators' are in a substantial majority.

The almost universal model adopted by system design metrics workers is based upon the idea of system complexity formulated by the architect Christopher Alexander.[4] This was adapted for software development in the functional design methodology of Stevens *et al.*;[195] in particular, it was incorporated in their design evaluation criteria of maximizing module cohesion and minimizing module coupling. Cohesion may be regarded as the singleness of purpose or function of a module. For example, a module that plays the national anthem and solves crosswords has a low cohesion because it performs two functions that are completely unrelated. This is generally considered to be an undesirable property of a module since it will result in it being harder to understand and more difficult to modify. In an informal sense we can predict that if a design comprises modules with low cohesion, this will result in various undesirable properties in the final product. In many ways coupling is the corollary of cohesion. It is the degree of independence of one module from another. Minimizing connections between modules makes them easier to understand and update.

Within this general framework, a number of different design metrics have been proposed. They differ mainly in the detail of how best to capture coupling and cohesion, and what notation they are best extracted from. Metrics either capture aspects of a design that are internal to individual modules — these we term *intra-modular design metrics* — or they deal with the relationships between modules — these we term *inter-modular design metrics* — or they deal with both. The following discussion deals with each family of design metrics in turn.

2.4.1 *Intra-modular design metrics*

The first family of metrics are those that deal solely with aspects of intra-modular complexity, and contain two exceptions to the general model described, in that they are extensions to Halstead's Software Science.[163, 202] These allow the designer to estimate the various measures such as η_1 and η_2 prior to the completion of code in order to calculate the Software Science metrics. Neither have been tested extensively, and both suffer from the inherent weaknesses of Halstead's model discussed earlier in this chapter.

Another metric in the intra-modular measurement family is Emerson's cohesion metric[54] based on module flow graphs and variable reference sets. The aim is to discriminate between the different types of module cohesion that Stevens *et al.*[195] describe. However, the metric is unvalidated, apart from the author's observation that the metric indicates high levels of cohesion for 25 published modules.[108] This is justified on the basis that the modules are intended as examples of 'good design' and, therefore, could reasonably be expected to be highly cohesive.

All the metrics in this family are severely disadvantaged by requiring knowledge of the internal details of each module in question. Unfortunately, this is unlikely to be available before coding is well under way — if not complete. Although such metrics may have a role, they cannot be considered true design metrics.

2.4.2 *Inter- and intra-modular design metrics*

The second family of design metrics are those based upon a combination of inter-modular and intra-modular measurements. The general rationale for this approach is that the total complexity of a design is a function of the sum of the individual complexities of each design component and the manner in which these components interrelate.

Probably the most widely known design metric in this family is the information flow measure,[81, 82, 83, 84, 103] which attempts to capture the structural complexity of a system, and to provide a specific, quantitative basis for design decision making. Henry and Kafura considered that the prime factor determining structural complexity was the connectivity of a module* to its environment. Relative to other design metrics, information flow is well tested. The empirical results are somewhat mixed, although the work of Shepperd and Ince[186] suggests that refinements to the basic model produce considerably improved results in terms of the ability to predict software quality factors of interest. A more detailed analysis of the underlying model is presented in the next chapter.

A similar metric has been proposed by Card and Agresti[31] which explicitly identifies total design complexity as comprising inter-modular or structural complexity plus the sum of all the intra-modular or local complexities. The structural complexity is given as the sum of the squares of individual module fan-outs. The fan-in factor is disregarded as previous empirical work[32] has shown it to be insignificant, coupled with the problem that counting it penalizes module reuse. Local complexity for a module is the number of imported and exported variables, divided by the fan-out plus one. The rationale for this is that the greater the number of arguments, the greater the module workload. On the other hand, the greater the module fan-out the greater the proportion of this workload that is distributed to other modules. Local complexities are then summed across the system.

An empirical analysis of this metric by its authors found a correspondence between their measure and a subjective design quality rating.[31] In addition, they also obtained a significant correlation between the metric and error density. An attempt to employ the local complexity metric as a means of measuring module size (in terms of ELOC, decision count and variable count) found the metric to be almost orthogonal to module size.[181, 186] This is a rather disturbing discovery. Plainly, much more empirical work is required before confidence can be placed in these metrics.

McClure[136] has argued that complexity accrues from the number of modules that modify control variables (those program variables that make up predicates for branching decisions). Ideally, control variables would be local to the module that utilizes them. Unfortunately, little evidence is proffered to support this hypothesis, other than a case study analysis of a small database management system where some relationship was found between the metric and subjective maintenance complexity.[104] From a design metric perspective there is the additional disadvantage that one would be unlikely to have an accurate picture of all the control variables, or their usage, until coding was well underway, thus making the metric difficult to obtain at design time.

---

*Strictly speaking, we should use the term 'procedure' since in Henry and Kafura's terminology 'module' is applied to the set of all procedures that reference a particular data structure. We will not do so in order to avoid suggestions of specific programming language dependence, and to keep to generally accepted nomenclature.

Another widely cited metric in this family is Yau and Collofello's stability metric[218, 217] which considers a design from the point of view of its resistance to change. In a poor design a simple maintenance change will ripple through a large number of modules. Conversely, a good design will contain the change within a single module. Clearly, a design that is made of decoupled cohesive modules will have low resistance to change.

Since maintenance tasks are so variable it is difficult to select a representative task with which to measure system stability. Yau and Collofello use a fundamental task, which, they argue, is common to all maintenance changes: that of a modifying a single variable. Module interface and global data structure information is required to calculate the inter-modular propagation of change. Additionally, detailed knowledge of the internal structure of each module is needed to calculate the intra-modular change propagation. As they observe, the metric cannot be used as the sole arbiter of good design since a single module of 20 000 LOC will contain most maintenance changes. However it may lead to many very undesirable side effects! Although an attempt has been made to infer the metric from solely design information,[104] the results were considered unreliable. So, it would appear that to calculate the worst case, ripple effect code is required. This is a major drawback to an otherwise novel and promising approach.

A more recent contribution is McCabe's family of design metrics,[135] which is calculated by examining the module calling hierarchy (inter-modular input) and module psuedo-code which describes the control flow of the module invocations. The approach is graph theoretic in an analogous fashion to better-known code metric counterparts such as cyclomatic complexity.[133] The metrics derived by McCabe are known as module design complexity, design complexity, and integration complexity. Each of these will be reviewed briefly.

Module design complexity, iv, is based upon the internal logic of a module as might be captured by pseudo-code. This can be depicted as a flow graph in the usual manner,[62, 133] and then reduced in order to arrive at a graph of only those paths that contain module invocations. Module design complexity is deemed to be the cyclomatic number of such a reduced graph. Consequently, all leaf modules will have an iv value of one.

Design complexity, S_o, is the sum of the module design complexities for a module and all its descendants, excepting modules that are called from more than one point within the design, in which case the module is only counted once.

Integration complexity is the basis set of module invocation sub-trees. McCabe uses the basis set, rather than the actual number of distinct sub-trees, since unbounded iterative module invocations lead to the latter being uncountable. His argument is — as with the code metric — that the basis set, when taken in linear combination, can yield all possible sub-trees and is therefore a good indicator of testing effort, or, in this case, integration testing effort.

It would seem that McCabe's main concern is that of testing and to that end he offers a 'structured integration testing methodology'.[135] Unfortunately, this leaves one a little unclear as to the meaning of the design metric S_o. The approach is interesting in that it recognizes that software testing effort is strongly dependent on structural features, but is possibly handicapped by the need for intra-modular information, thus delaying its availability. The absence of any published empirical support for the metrics must also be regarded as disappointing.

2.4.3 Inter-modular design metrics

The third and final family of design metrics consists of those based purely upon inter-modular considerations. The simplest of these is a metric developed by Yin and Winchester and based on graph impurity.[219] Their complexity metric is based upon the design notation of a module hierarchy chart extended to include global data structure access information. This is treated as a graph (or network). Design complexity is deemed to be a function of how far the network departs from a pure tree (i.e. its graph impurity). Essentially, this metric measures the complexity of connections within a design, and gives a crude indication of module coupling. Figure 2.1 shows a simple example, where the graph impurity metric C_i' is defined as

$$C_i' = A_i' - T_i' \tag{2.1}$$

where N_i' is the number of modules and data structures from L_0 to L_i; T_i' is the number of module and data structure tree arcs from L_0 to L_i (i.e. $N_i' - 1$); and A_i' is the number of module and data structure network arcs from L_0 to L_i. Although the designer should seek to minimize C_i' where a choice exists, this should not override the reuse of components where possible. The other application of this metric is to examine trends between levels within a hierarchy, as with the Henry and Kafura information flow metric.

A validation of C_i' against two projects at the Hughes Corporation produced a high positive correlation between the metric and the error count. As Yin and Winchester note, this was in part due to the effect of a small number of outlier modules on the correlation. Once these were removed a correlation coefficient of $r = 0.52$ was obtained. This indicated that the metric has some statistical significance but cannot fully 'explain' the error count. In many ways this is not surprising: the metric is based on a very naïve model which assumes that departure from a pure tree structure is the major determinant of complexity. In the authors' opinion it is more likely that the graph impurity is a proxy for size (i.e. strongly dependent), particularly since the metric is not normalized for size, and therefore what is being observed is an example of cross-correlation.

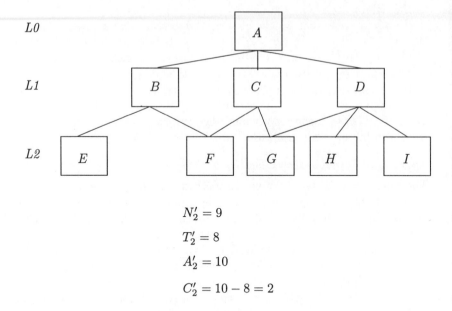

$$N'_2 = 9$$
$$T'_2 = 8$$
$$A'_2 = 10$$
$$C'_2 = 10 - 8 = 2$$

FIG. 2.1. An example of a graph impurity measurement.

Another graph-based metric has been proposed by Benyon-Tinker[22] based on his study of a large commercial software system written in Algol. Again, modules are represented by nodes and calls by edges. In this case the assumption is made that if a module is invoked more than once this need not be reflected by the metric because the module, or, strictly, the sub-graph representing it, has already been analysed and, presumably, understood. Thus, the graph of what Benyon-Tinker called *distinct nodes* will, in fact, be a pure tree since whenever a module is invoked for a second or nth time this will not be incorporated into the graph.

The Benyon-Tinker metric C for a whole program is given by:

$$num = \sum_{r=1}^{m} n_r * r^\alpha \tag{2.2}$$

$$den = \sum_{r=1}^{m} n_r \tag{2.3}$$

$$C = \frac{num}{den} \tag{2.4}$$

where n_r is the number of distinct nodes at level r, m is the maximum depth of the tree, and α is a power law index.

Complexity is a function of the depth and breadth of the tree. Benyon-Tinker's study led him to suggest that values for α, the power law index, should lie in the range 2–3.

The empirical evidence to support this metric is based upon subjective evaluation. Benyon-Tinker used the metric to identify potentially problematic modules which he then found corresponded well with the user's subjective, but well-informed, judgement. Although this constitutes a basis for validation, it cannot be considered sufficient in its own right.

Adopting, a slightly different approach, though still based upon inter-modular measurements, is Chapin's Q metric.[34] This metric not only uses the inputs and outputs to each module (i.e. the module interface) but also attempts to give a weighting factor dependent on the purpose of the data, since this influences the complexity of the module interface. The following types of data are identified:

P_m inputs required for processing;
M_m inputs that are modified by the execution of the module;
C_m inputs that control decisions or selections;
T_m through data that is transmitted unchanged.

Module complexity is calculated as:

$$Q_m = (3 * C_m + 2 * M_m + P_m + 0.5 * T_m) * (1 + (E/3)^2) \qquad (2.5)$$

where E is a term that represents the additional complexity that accrues when a module communicates with another and is invoked iteratively. E is zero, except where a module contains the exit test for an iteratively invoked module. For each C data item that is imported and used in the iteration exit test, E is incremented by one if it originates from a subordinate module, and by two if it is from a non-subordinate module.

Although the different weights are rather arbitrary they could be refined by careful empirical analysis. The main problem is the usual one of a complete lack of empirical validation, coupled with the difficulty of automation since the interface data has to be categorized manually.

Beane et al.[18] also propose a metric based upon module connections and, additionally, suggest a design notation from which the necessary measurements may be culled. This is a special purpose design language called a Component Interaction Language (CIL), which can be used to describe the structural aspects of a design in a hierarchical manner.

From this information a number of metrics can be generated at an early stage of the software life-cycle in order to alert the designer to possible problem areas, to make comparisons between alternative designs, and to predict development effort. Beane et al. suggest two metrics of particular interest:

- the stress point metric: the number of direct connections to a part, divided by the mean number of connections per part — the direction of the connection being ignored;

- the path metric: the sum of all path lengths through the system or area of interest including indirect connections.

A small, subjective case study validation suggested that these two metrics can be applied in conjunction with a variety of design methodologies. The most convincing use was found to be as an evaluation tool comparing alternative design solutions.

An approach that is rather different from the previous metrics is based upon an exploratory data analysis technique known as *cluster analysis*. The technique attempts to group objects together on the basis of similarity, so that most similar objects will be grouped together first. The output is usually a dendogram or cluster tree which reveals the order of clustering. A number of researchers[21, 87, 91, 94, 171] have tried to harness this method towards the generation of some idealized module hierarchy based upon the principle of grouping the most similar modules that are closest together within the module hierarchy. The usual indicator of similarity has been taken to be module couplings or shared information flows. Although this is an intriguing idea, there is a long way to go before this class of metric reaches maturity. Possibly the greatest stumbling block is that the shape of the dendogram is highly dependant upon the choice of clustering algorithm.

The validity of concentrating upon inter-modular measures, and connections in particular, has been strengthened considerably by the empirical work of Troy and Zweben.[204] Their study of 73 designs and associated implementations indicated that those measures relating to module coupling were most effective at predicting the incidence of errors. These included the number and type of module interconnections and the number of global data structure references. This forms the basis of the majority of design metrics reviewed above.

2.5   Specification metrics

The benefits of design metrics, in that they provide early feedback about the developing software product, are even stronger for metrics derived from product specifications. However, the difficulties are greater and research in this field is less well advanced.

Prominent in this field are the ideas of Albrecht and Gaffney.[2, 3] During the mid-1970s, while working at IBM, he evolved an alternative approach to assessing the 'size' of a piece of software based upon the level of functionality provided. This led to a simple metric based upon a count of 'function points'. These are derived by means of an analysis of the requirements specification document in order to identify the different functions that the system is to perform. The functions are classified into different types, and given weightings according to the relative complexity of the

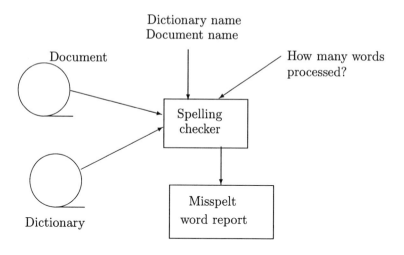

2 external files
2 input types   =4*2+5*1+4*1+7*2
1 enquiry   = 31 function points
1 output type

FIG. 2.2. Function point analysis of a simple spelling checker.

function type. For example, Albrecht considered interfacing with external systems to be more complex than processing queries. The unadjusted function point count ufc for a specification is given by:

$$4 * i + 5 * o + 4 * e + 7 * p + 10 * f$$

where:

i is the number of external input types
o is the number of external output types
e is the number of enquiries
p is the number of external files (program interfaces)
f is the number of internal files

Note that the equation is simplified in that it does give the adjustments for function type complexity. A detailed account of how to determine function type complexity can be found in Albrecht and Gaffney.[3] Consider the example of a simple spelling checker in Figure 2.2. The function point metric can be extracted from the following simple specification:

The checker accepts a document file as input and lists all the words that are not contained in a dictionary file. The user is able to query the number of words processed whilst the checking is in progress, a feature which is useful when long documents are being examined. It is important to avoid counting items twice, thus in this example *Dictionary* is not treated as an input type because it is accounted for as an external file.

Having computed an unadjusted function point count, Albrecht suggests that a total of 14 technical complexity factors be taken into account. The factors are listed below:

Data communications	On-line update
Distributed data processing	Complex processing
Performance	Reusability
Heavily used configuration	Installation ease
Transaction rate	Operation ease
On-line data entry	Multiple sites
End user efficiency	Facilitate change

Each factor is scored between zero (no influence) and five (very strong influence). An overall technical complexity factor tcf is calculated as follows:

$$tcf = 0.65 + 0.01 * \sum DI_i$$

where DI_i is the degree of influence of the ith technical complexity factor. Thus tcf will range from 0.65 to 1.35. For a system characterized by simple processing, based upon a single processor without data communications, the value will tend towards 0.65. At the other end of the spectrum, a distributed system, dealing with high transaction volumes and characterized by complex processing, will tend towards 1.35. Combining the technical complexity factor and unadjusted function point count, we obtain the adjusted function point count:

$$fp = ufc * tcf$$

The function point metric is usually used as a predictor of development effort, although its inverse is often also used as a productivity index. For useful predictions to be made, function points require calibration so that they are converted into units of interest such as person days of effort. Since organizations and software development environments differ so widely, this is best done at a local level.[107]

Function points have been used at a number of different sites with some success,[19] and, once calibrated, have been found to be able to 'explain' 75% of the variation in program size in a study of 15 commercial software systems.[107] There are drawbacks, however. The weightings in the formula might be appropriate for IBM in the 1970s, but may well need considerable modification in the 1990s according to the type of application, experience and ability of the software developers, the development environment, and the programming language.

Since the early work of Albrecht, considerable effort has been devoted to standardizing function point counting practices under the auspices of the International Function Point Users Group (IFPUG), who have published a detailed set of counting procedures.[95] None the less, identifying functions from the specification can be a rather subjective process, particularly if working from an informal and unstructured specification (e.g. where excessive reliance is placed upon natural language). Low and Jeffery[129] report a typical level of 30% variation in counting points, from an experiment based upon 22 analysts working with an identical specification.

Notwithstanding these difficulties the metric has been adopted by a considerable number of commercial organizations, although this has tended to be most successful when structured specification techniques, such as data flow diagramming, are employed, coupled with a very stable measurement environment. The main weaknesses are the need for calibration, its unsuitability for the real-time domain, and doubt over the usefulness of the technical complexity adjustment.[107]

A number of variants of Albrecht's original approach have emerged. Symons has developed Mark II function points, which are best suited for information systems and are most easily derived from entity–relationship models.[200, 201] The CCTA* recommends their use in an SSADM development environment.[33] Other adaptations include those by Jones[100] and Reifer[162] for use in real-time environments. However, their ideas have yet to be subjected to much external validation.

A more sophisticated approach to specification metrics is provided by DeMarco's Bang metric,[47] which is derived from more formal specification notations (data flow diagrams, data dictionaries, entity relationship diagrams, and state transition diagrams), thereby simplifying the measuring process. DeMarco attempts to classify software as either 'function-strong', e.g. a robotics system, or 'data-strong', e.g. an information retrieval system. In order to make this distinction more objective, deMarco suggests that it be based upon a ratio between two counts. First, the number of relationships R are identified in the data model, usually depicted as an entity–relationship diagram, where the relationships are arrows linking entities or objects such as customer or invoice. Second, the count of primitive functions F identified in the data flow diagrams is calculated. This gives a categorization:

$R/F < 0.7$ is a function-strong system
$R/F \leq 1.5$ is a hybrid system

---

*The CCTA is a British organization responsible for government computing.

$R/F > 1.5$ is a data-strong system

The 'function-strong' system metric is derived from a count of primitive functions extracted from data flow diagrams. On its own this is unlikely to be satisfactory, since individual functions vary markedly in size and complexity depending upon their task. This can be compensated for by a table of weightings that allow for variations in size and type of function. This might range from 0.3 for a function that channels data according to some selection criteria, through 1.0 for a data management function, to 2.5 for a device management function. In addition, the size of a function will be dependent upon the number of data flows into and out of a function. Thus the size for function i, is given by:

$$SIZE_i = complexity_i(flows_i * \log flows_i) \tag{2.6}$$

and system size by:

$$size = \sum_{i=1}^{F} modification * RE_i \tag{2.7}$$

where F is the number of functions.

The 'data-strong' system metric is calculated from the count of relationships per entity (RE). This count is modified by the number of relationships that each entity has with other entities. This modification is non-linear so that an entity with four relationships is more than twice that of an entity with only two relationships. System size is given by:

$$size = \sum_{i=1}^{E} modification * RE_i \tag{2.8}$$

where E is the number of entities.

Hybrid systems present more of a problem. The obvious approach of combining the 'function-strong' and 'data-strong' calculations is flawed due to the intrinsic difficulty of mixing two dissimilar measures. DeMarco argues that the most satisfactory solution is to calculate both measures but keep them separate, and partition the project into those activities that relate to system function and those that relate to the system database.

Despite the intuitive appeal of deMarco's Bang metric there is no published empirical support for it. This may in part be because of the need for considerable tailoring of the metric to particular environments for which large bases of historical development data are required. It is also based upon specific notations for system requirements, in the absence of which the Bang metric cannot be applied. Not unnaturally, the metric is also dependent upon the quality of the inputs. Unsatisfactory and inaccurate data flow or entity–relationship diagrams inevitably lead to poor results. Nevertheless, for some software development environments, the Bang metric could offer useful assistance.

Samson *et al.*[167] take the logical step of attempting to derive useful measurements from OBJ, a formal specification notation, thus avoiding any of the ambiguities and problems of less formal techniques. Studying a small set of modules they found significant relationships between the number of equations required to define an operator on an abstract data type, and the cyclomatic complexity and length of the final implementation. Unfortunately, the very small size of the empirical validation renders it rather unconvincing, especially when coupled to the observation that a given specification may be expressed in a variety of ways in OBJ, although they could all be implemented by an identical piece of software.* Although the idea of measuring formal specifications may have potential, particularly if it can be used to predict other, more useful, product characteristics than the cyclomatic number, it will almost certainly be limited by the infrequent use of formal specification techniques within the software industry. chapter has provided a fairly brief overview of the last three decades of product metrics research and development. It has described some of the key works in the large volume of work that has been carried out, and has provided a number of indications of the major problems afflicting the metrics area. These problems are: the continuous use of terms such as 'complexity' and 'quality' without any attempts at definition; the formulation of metrics in a very unclear way; minimal levels of empirical validation; and an almost obsessive concentration on code metrics rather than metrics which can be extracted at an early point in the software project. The following chapter expands on these hints by looking at deficiencies in three well-known, much cited metrics, and demonstrates that the problems are very serious.

---

*A point vividly brought home to one of the authors when trying to develop OBJ specifications in an MSDOS environment, making it necessary to 'shoe horn' the specification into a minimal set of equations. An initial specification comprised of 65 equations was eventually reduced to 33 without making behavioural changes to the system.

3

PROMISES AND PROBLEMS

Synopsis

This chapter examines the metrics of the Software Science model,[75] cyclomatic complexity,[133] and information flow[82] in more detail. These are selected on the basis of their popularity within the software engineering literature, and the significance of the claims made by their progenitors. Claimed benefits are summarized. Each metric is then made the subject of an in-depth critique and all are found wanting. The important point made by this chapter is that this is not due to mischance, but is indicative of deeper problems of methodology employed in the field of software metrics.

3.1 Introduction

The preceding chapter has provided an introduction to the area of software metrics and has, at the same time, outlined some of the major problems of the subject. The aim of this chapter is to look at three widely used metrics and use them as examples to illustrate more fully these problems. The first metric — or rather family of metrics — is that derived from Halstead's Software Science which is almost certainly the widest studied and 'validated' metric. Of the three metrics examined in this chapter this has, over the last ten years, been the recipient of most criticism; we summarize these criticisms here.

The second metric, cyclomatic complexity, is due to McCabe.[133] As with the work of Halstead the application of the cyclomatic complexity metric, and its related offshoots, has been far-ranging. It is difficult to underestimate the impact of McCabe's work, and today the creation, investigation, and promulgation of graph-theoretic software measures is a major industry. Yet, surprisingly, the usefulness of cyclomatic complexity as a software metric has been allowed to pass relatively unquestioned. Indeed it is still widely cited in textbooks,[5, 161, 190, 211] subjected to many minor 'tinkerings',[78, 96, 143, 188, 191, 216] and applied as a design metric.[73] Yet, its empirical basis would, at present, appear to remarkably sparse and its theoretical underpinning extremely suspect.

A more recent contender is the information flow metric due to Sallie Henry and Denis Kafura.[82, 84] This metric has achieved a great deal of prominence. It may be extracted from a system design, and is thus available far earlier than code metrics. The authors claim that it may be used for prediction, and also to pinpoint weaknesses in a system architecture, thereby providing much needed feedback during the design process. Furthermore, it is virtually the only early life-cycle metric to have received any serious empirical validation. Consequently, it is almost inevitably cited in current papers on system design measurement.*

The three metrics: Software Science, cyclomatic complexity, and information flow, have therefore been selected as being representative of a great deal of current work in the software metrics domain. Moreover, much additional work treats these metrics and their underlying models as fundamental. In addition, these metrics are the most widely applied, generating a considerable amount of empirical evidence. The approach has been adopted that since these metrics may reasonably be regarded as typical it is appropriate to subject them to more detailed scrutiny, and that findings relating to these metrics may be treated as representative of the field.

This chapter will reveal a constant pattern of poorly conceived models that underlie the three metrics examined. This has lead, in turn, to metrics which are anomalous and out of step with current software engineering practice. What the chapter also demonstrates is that the lowly role given to modelling has given rise to many problems in validation. In short, this chapter reveals major weaknesses in foundation and methodology.

Before looking at the three metrics in detail it is worth stressing that this chapter is not meant to be a destructive criticism of the metrics and their developers. Each metric and its associated research marks a landmark in the history of software metrics: Software Science was the first attempt to erect a theory of software measurement; cyclomatic complexity alerted the software community to the possibilities of measuring the unstructuredness of program code; and the work of Sally Henry and Dennis Kafura pointed out the importance of measuring inter-module factors. This chapter attempts to dissect the work, with the results of the dissection being used to construct a method for developing and validating metrics which is described in Chapters 5 – 7.

3.2 Software science

Halstead's so called Software Science[75] — originally called Software Physics — was one of the earliest attempts to provide a code metric based on a coherent model of software complexity.[66, 74, 128, 206] The underlying idea behind Software Science is that software comprehension is a process of mental manipulation of program tokens. These tokens can be characterized as operators (executable program verbs such as IF, DIV, and READ) or

---

*Even Navlakha's perfunctory survey of design metrics[145] managed to include reference to the work of Henry and Kafura.

operands (variables and constants). Given this division a program can be regarded as a sequence of operators and their associated operands.

The Software Science metrics are derived from the following counts:

η_1 = count of unique operators
η_2 = count of unique operands
N_1 = total no. of operators
N_2 = total no. of operands

The program vocabulary, η, is given by:

$$\eta = \eta_1 + \eta_2 \tag{3.1}$$

and the program length, N, in tokens, by:

$$N = N_1 + N_2 \tag{3.2}$$

Halstead suggested that manipulation of a token — an operand or operator — requires retrieval from some sort of mental dictionary that consists of the entire program vocabulary η. He also suggested that this retrieval is achieved by means of a binary search mechanism. Given this, the number of mental comparisons, or dictionary accesses, required to understand the piece of software can be calculated from the size of the vocabulary and the total number of tokens that are used. This is known as the program volume V, it is defined as:

$$V = N * \log n \tag{3.3}$$

Because a program may be programmed in a number of different ways, it is useful to have a measure of a particular implementation's volume compared with some theoretical optimum solution with minimum volume, V^*. This is known as the program level λ:

$$\lambda = V^*/V \tag{3.4}$$

Another metric is one that indicates increasing difficulty, known as D, and is the inverse of program level:

$$D = 1/\lambda \tag{3.5}$$

Normally it is impossible to derive the potential volume V^*, so an estimate of the program level, $\hat{\lambda}$, is used:

$$\hat{\lambda} = (2/\eta_1) * (\eta_2/N_2) \tag{3.6}$$

Similarly, the estimated difficulty metric, $\hat{D}$, is:

$$\hat{D} = (\eta_1/2) * (N_2/\eta_2) \qquad (3.7)$$

The rationale for equation (3.7) is as follows. The term $(\eta_1/2)$ will increase with the use of additional operators and, therefore, adds to the complexity of the code. The divisor is 2 because this is the minimum possible number of operators required to implement a particular algorithm: a function call and a function argument.* The term (N_2/η_2) is the average use of an operand.

Given that the level of program difficulty gives the number of elementary mental discriminations (EMD) per comparison, and that the volume gives the total number of comparisons, it is possible to produce a figure for the effort E required to manipulate the program:

$$E = D * V \qquad (3.8)$$

A major assumption of the Halstead model is that programmers make a constant number of EMDs per unit time. Using research carried out by the cognitive psychologist Stroud,[196] Halstead suggested that the time T required to generate the program could be calculated by using the Stroud number S, which is the number of EMDs the brain is able to make per second.† Stroud's original estimate of S was that it was within the range 5 – 20. Halstead, using a value of S equal to 18, was able to predict T in seconds as:

$$T = E/18 \qquad (3.9)$$

Halstead also derived an equation for estimating program length $\hat{N}$. This only used the counts η_1 and η_2 that are available prior to completion of coding. Thus, we have:

$$\hat{N} = \eta_1 * \log \eta_1 + \eta_2 * \log \eta_2 \qquad (3.10)$$

Halstead hypothesized that, for a particular programming language, as V^* increases the program level λ will decrease such that $V*L$ remains invariant. Using this invariant, which he termed l or the language level, values were obtained of 1.53 for PL/1, 1.21 for ALGOL, 1.14 for FORTRAN and 0.88 for CDC assembly language.[75] There have been a number of wide-ranging

---

*This justification for estimated difficulty, $\hat{D}$, is restricted to those programming languages which support procedure invocation and parameter passing. As a consequence, Software Science has a more limited domain than some of its proponents claim, e.g. van der Kniff.[206]

†Unfortunately, Halstead took Stroud's work rather out of context and, in addition, adopted a value that lies very much at the top of the range of values suggested by Stroud. This theme will be developed further in the critique of Halstead's work in the next chapter.

attempts to establish this metric for other languages, for example, ESS,[8] COBOL,[174, 224] PL/S and BAL,[189] RPG,[80] and APL.[224, 122]

A feature apparent in all the above investigations is that, with the exception of APL, which produced a surprisingly low value of λ, the results accord with intuitive expectations. However, more careful analysis reveals large variances and a strong inverse dependence on length.[77, 173] It has been suggested by Christensen et al.[37] that what is being captured is not the language level, but the use of the language by the programmer. These major misgivings have not prevented further work in this area.[116, 117, 207]

Early empirical validations of Software Science produced apparently* large correlations between predicted and actual results. Studies have related Software Science measures to development time,[70, 75] to the incidence of software bugs,[66] program recall,[127] and program quality.[53, 64, 128] Software Science metrics have even been used to detect student plagiarism.[147] Extending the educational application possibilities still further, Shen investigated the relationship between Software Science and student grades.[172] It has also been suggested that the effort metric, E could be used as a measure of good programming practice,[69] on the basis that E was reduced 40 times out of 46 in examples of 'improved' programs culled from Kernighan and Plauger's classic work on programming style.[108] Subsequent work has been rather less positive.

Software Science attracted considerable interest in the 1970s because of the novelty of measuring software then. Also, the basic inputs measurements for the metric are all easily extracted automatically. A Pascal program to extract the Software Science metrics reproduced in deMarco's well known metrics text book[47] is scarcely 200 lines long.

Despite the initial enthusiastic reception for Software Science, a number of serious problems has recently emerged. Since Halstead published his work, software engineers have carried out multifarious attempts at empirical validation of these metrics. However, careful analysis of the results reveal a number of disturbing problems. These are summarized in Table 3.1. It is worth stating that the final column of this table represents a subjective judgement by the authors. A threshold of $r^2 = 0.4$, modified by considerations of experimental quality, has been adopted. The WEAK classification is applied where the correlation is statistically significant but does not meet the above criterion. First, different researchers have applied the metric to a large number of different software attributes, ranging through ease of maintenance, number of errors, program recall, and development time, to documentation effort. This results in difficulties in comparison of work and evaluation of the metric, since it is unclear precisely what the

---

*Careful review of the methods and analytical techniques employed, for example by Hamer and Frewin,[77] suggest that these correlations are less significant than was first believed

Table 3.1 *Empirical validations of Software Science*

Study	Correlation with LOC	Better than LOC?	Dependent variable	Useful predictor?
13	n.a.	=	effort	WEAK
17	n.a.	NO	bug location	WEAK
17	n.a.	NO	effort	WEAK
27	n.a.	NO	errors	NO
27	n.a.	NO	bug location	NO
42	YES	NO	program recall	NO
43	YES	YES	bug location	YES
53	n.a.	n.a.	length	YES
56	n.a.	n.a.	program style	NO
66	n.a.	n.a.	errors	NO
65	n.a.	n.a.	debugging effort	NO
70	n.a.	n.a.	effort	YES
75	n.a.	n.a.	effort	NO
84	YES	n.a.	changes	YES
123	YES	NO	effort	WEAK
148	n.a.	n.a.	debugging effort	NO
172	YES	NO	effort	NO
213	n.a.	n.a.	effort	WEAK

metric is addressing, or if it is intended as a General Model of Software which is capable of predicting almost any aspect of software on the basis of program operand and operator counts. Kearney *et al.*[106] outline some of the difficulties inherent in such an approach. Factors that reduce development effort may not result in more reliable and maintainable software.

Second, even where there is agreement as to which aspect of software engineering Halstead's metrics are addressing, they and many of their associated empirical validations encounter problems of what exactly to include within the ambit of their studies. For example, what is meant by development time? Does this include time spent analysing requirements or time spent upon design work? Should effort expended on documentation be included? What about the scenario in which the developer lies awake at night pondering some particularly intractable problem? These issues are not addressed by Software Science because the underlying model is couched in terms that are too nebulous to admit more precise definition.

Third, a seemingly simple task as counting operands and operators is fraught with difficulties. This is because Halstead relied upon an intuitive understanding of these concepts. Clearly, this is not adequate, particularly for the primary input to the metric. This alone should cause us to treat empirical results with a certain degree of caution. A more formal definition is required of these counts, together with the mapping process from code to the metric.

Fourth, there is considerable disquiet concerning the quality of many empirical validations and their associated statistical analyses. Hamer and Frewin[77] have re-examined the experimental data from two studies[38, 75] that claim high correlations between E and actual programming time. They report that coding time is not proportional to E, rather that it is proportional to the square root of E. Even applying this relationship, however, still yields an unacceptable level of inaccuracy. They also reveal flaws in Halstead's approach to larger systems, as on certain occasions the E metric was obtained by calculating the metric for individual modules and summing across the system.* On other occasions the metric was obtained by treating a system as a single module.† As Hamer and Frewin note, this 'minor' error results in a 20-fold overestimate of effort required, and thus casts a rather substantial shadow over the claimed confirmation. Parenthetically, we note, this type of error is unsurprising, given the extremely restricted view of software that Halstead's model embodies, being originally concerned only with trivial FORTRAN algorithms. It is also unfortunate that the majority of studies deal with very small-scale programs and use non-professional programmers — in one case a single student.[70]

Discrepancies have also been identified by Hamer and Frewin in the analyses of Funayami and Halstead[66] and Ottenstein[148] which were derived from the same source, *viz* Akiyama's debugging data. The Funami study used mis-reported data and incorrectly estimated η_1 and η_2 but, nevertheless, obtained a high correlation with the actual debugging data. By contrast, Ottenstein applied the Software Science model correctly and obtained results that did not agree with the actual data; as a consequence she multiplied her estimates by a project-dependent constant in a manner entirely inconsistent with the Software Science model.‡

Card and Agresti[30] also argue that many of the impressive empirical results supporting Software Science are more apparent than real. More specifically, they show that the high correlations found between estimated and actual program length are a consequence of the fact that N and $\hat{N}$ are dependent by definition, thus a positive correlation must exist.

In addition to questionable empirical support there are a number of theoretical objections. First, there are serious problems with the definitions of operators η_1 and operands η_2. Many of Halstead's counting rules appear rather arbitrary; it is not obvious why all input/output and declar-

---

*This is the approach advised in what may be taken as Halstead's definitive work.[75]

†This is the approach adopted to analyse the Walston and Felix data taken from 60 IBM projects, and also presented in[75] as a major confirmation of Software Science.

‡Hamer and Frewin[77] present a table comparing the different results. This seems to have excited no comment other than that both studies lend support to Halstead's work. Clearly, such support is entirely illusory.

ative statements should be ignored, particularly as in many languages this can be a significant part of the total development effort; for example a COBOL programmer may not be in full agreement with the view that all non-Procedure-Division statements are mere 'syntactic sugar'![147] The treatment of goto <label> as a unique operator for each unique label is quite inconsistent with the treatment of if <condition> as a single operator irrespective of the number of unique conditions.[121] Overloaded operators cause further problems, for example in a language like Ada. These counting problems are significant because Software Science metrics are sensitive to rule changes,[23, 173] which is rather disturbing since it implies that results are dependent on arbitrary decisions rather than on the underlying model.*

A second area of objection involves the psychological assumptions that the model makes. The volume metric is suspect given the lack of empirical evidence for a binary search mechanism within the context of programming.[40] Just as serious, given its potential use for software engineers, are the problems with the time equation

$$T = E/S \qquad (3.11)$$

where S is the so called Stroud number, after the psychologist Stroud.[196] Stroud stated that:

> there are approximately *ten* moments of psychological time for every second of physical time, though there may be more; as many as twenty, or less, or few as five.[†]

The adoption of a value of 18 for S, despite the fact that it improves correlation coefficients,[75] must be regarded as arbitrary. Furthermore, Stroud's studies were confined to sensory memory, and there is no good reason to suppose that computer programming can be treated in the same way. Indeed, there are a number of more recent models that would suggest otherwise. Apart, from Halstead's work[75] and a study by Ottenstein,[148] there has been little other validation of the conjecture $S = 18$. Zweben and Fung[224] report difficulties with S and question the assumption that it is constant.

Third, the view of software as a sequence of tokens is very simplistic: it ignores control structure, program structure, and data structure. Lassez *et al.*[121] point out that for many programming languages, operators and operands cannot be considered to be mutually exclusive, as, for example, in the use of procedure calls as parameters. They dispute that such a

---

*The dangers inherent in such a situation are well illustrated by the decision of Balut *et al.*[10] to treat each goto as a unique operator without justification, other than that it improved the correspondence between N and $\hat{N}$. The consequence of this *ad hoc* decision was the introduction of new anomalies into Software Science.

[†]Stroud is quoted by Coulter;[40] the emphasis is ours.

simple characterization of software is an appropriate model, and argue that a distinction should be made between operators that control flow and those that are more functional in nature such as + and div. The Johnston and Lister[99] study of Pascal software and a subsequent critique[126] of Halstead indicate that the lack of distinction causes problems — at least in some domains.

Finally, there are difficulties that relate to the scale of the software. The original work was concerned with small-scale algorithms, for example the experiments of Gordon and Halstead[70] deal with programs of between 7 and 59 statements, as opposed to large-scale software systems. Therein lies the problem. One of the main tenets of software engineering is that large-scale software does not exhibit similar properties to its small scale counterpart.

Although to Halstead's credit he did attempt to postulate an underlying model for Software Science, many of the psychological and software engineering assumptions have been challenged and shown to be without foundation. Moreover, what upon first sight appears to have been an impregnable empirical position has also been found wanting. In particular, many experiments have been shown to be unrepresentative have produced few data points, have generated results based upon inappropriate statistical techniques, and have been incapable of refuting the hypothesis under examination. It is also noteworthy that, for a significant number of studies, Software Science measures have performed no better than LOC metrics. Given the serious criticisms that have been levelled at Software Science, its role within software engineering seems to be very limited, especially as a universal model of program complexity. Despite these difficulties there remains widespread and uncritical reference to it, even in the recent literature and text books.[5, 160, 168] Nevertheless, given the absence of a clear pattern in the empirical analyses described above, one must have misgivings concerning the model and its application. Possibly the most important legacy of Software Science is in the way that it attempts to provide a coherent and explicit model of program complexity as a framework within which to measure and make interpretations. Conte et al.[39] provide a fitting epitaph for Halstead's work:

> Halstead's work was instrumental in making metric studies an issue with computer scientists. Although the model of the programming process he proposed has limited empirical support, his work suggested that it was possible to apply a scientific approach to the programming process which for years had been considered an art.

Nevertheless, Halstead's pioneering work is valuable in that throws down a challenge: to reformulate its basic philosophy, after a more precise identification of the phenomenology and process.

3.3 Cyclomatic complexity

At about the same time as Halstead was researching Software Science, an alternative measure of software complexity known as cyclomatic complexity was proposed by McCabe,[133] who was particularly interested in the number of control flow paths through a piece of software, since this appeared to be related to testing difficulty and to the most effective way of dividing software into modules. Even at this juncture the dual, and not necessarily complementary, aims of McCabe's metric should be underlined.

Programs can be represented as directed graphs to show the control flow. From a graph G the cyclomatic complexity $v(G)$ can be extracted. This is the number of basic paths within the graph: the minimum set of paths which can be used to construct all other paths through the graph. The cyclomatic complexity is also equivalent to the number of decisions plus one within a program.

McCabe saw a practical application of the metric in using it to provide an upper limit to module complexity, beyond which a module should be sub-divided into simpler components. A value of $v(G)$ of 10 was suggested, although it was accepted that in certain situations — notably large case structures — the limit might be relaxed.

Like Software Science, McCabe's metric was well received by the software engineering community and became the subject of innumerable minor variations and empirical studies. Also, like Software Science, the metric has been widely interpreted as a general measure of software complexity, able to predict any facet of software or software development that is even remotely linked to complexity.

Unfortunately, we are confronted with an underlying model which is almost completely vacuous. In essence, it is that almost all software properties are in some way linked to the number of decisions contained within the program code. Careful analysis of the model reveals anomalous behaviour, particularly with respect to modularization,[176] and widely accepted principles of good programming practice.[55, 56] Again, the metric relies upon our intuitive understanding of what constitutes a decision. A number of significant counting issues have been thrown up in practice which illustrate the deficiency of the metric, and the need for a more formal mapping from a program to its flow graph. Furthermore, even if the empirical evidence is accepted at face value — though it is arguable that it should not — the case for cyclomatic complexity is remarkably unconvincing. In many cases it is out-performed by the straightforward lines of code metric LOC.[109, 208]

The rather simplistic view of software complexity that McCabe put forward can be challenged on a number of points. First, he was chiefly concerned with FORTRAN programs where the mapping from code to a program flow graph is well defined. This is not the case for other languages such as Ada. For example, it is unclear how an implicit exception event handling construct can be adequately represented by flow graphs.

A second type of objection is that $v(G) = 1$ will remain true for a linear sequence of code of any length. Consequently, the metric is insensitive to complexity contributed from linear sequences of statements. Some workers suggest that software can be categorized as either decision-bound or function-bound.[84] The function-bound software represents a major class of systems for which the metric is a poor predictor.

A third difficulty is the insensitivity of cyclomatic complexity to the structuring of software. A number of researchers[9, 149, 158, 188] have demonstrated that cyclomatic complexity can increase when applying generally accepted techniques to improve program structure. Evangelist[55, 56] reports that the application of only two out of 26 of Kernighan and Plauger's rules of good programming style[108] results in all cases in a decrease in cyclomatic complexity.

It could be claimed that this argument is a specific case of a more general point that the metric ignores the context or environment of each decision. All decisions have a uniform weight, regardless of depth of nesting or relationship with other decisions. In other words, McCabe takes a lexical rather than a structural view. Modifications have been proposed that allow for nesting depth.[132, 156, 158]

A fourth objection to cyclomatic complexity is inconsistent behaviour when measuring modularized software. It has been demonstrated that cyclomatic complexity increases with the addition of extra modules, but decreases with the factoring out of duplicate code.[176] All other aspects of modularity are disregarded. This is contrary to current ideas of correct modularization, and causes problems with respect to McCabe's objective of helping the designer to select an effective software architecture.

The difficulties described so far could be termed theoretical, but the empirical evidence is no more encouraging. Many of the early metric validations were based solely upon intuitive notions of complexity, for example McCabe stated that 'the complexity measure $v(G)$ is designed to conform to our intuitive notion of complexity'. Hansen states that a good measure of program complexity should satisfy several criteria including that of relating 'intuitively to the psychological complexity of programs'. He does not suggest that there is a need for any objective validation. Likewise, Myers[143] treated intuition as sufficient grounds for employing the metric.

This strikes us as a rather curious approach in that if intuition is a reliable arbiter of complexity, this eliminates the need for a quantitative measure. On the other hand, if intuition cannot be relied upon, it hardly provides a reasonable basis for validation. Clearly, a more objective approach to validation is required.

The metric is also vulnerable to the criticism that it ignores other aspects of software such as data and functional complexity. It is easy to construct certain pathological examples. However, this need not invalidate

Table 3.2 *Empirical validations of cyclomatic complexity*

Study	Correlation with LOC	Better than LOC?	Dependent variable	Useful predictor?
17	n.a.	n.a.	bug location	No
17	n.a.	n.a.	effort	No
12	Yes	n.a.	error density	No
27	n.a.	n.a.	errors	Weak
27	n.a.	n.a.	bug location	No
42	Yes	No	program recall	No
43	Yes	n.a.	bug location	Weak
67	n.a.	n.a.	effort	Yes
84	Yes	n.a.	changes	Yes
109	Yes	No	errors	Weak
123	Yes	No	effort	Weak
151	Yes	No	testing effort	Weak
168	Yes	n.a.	errors	No
175	n.a.	n.a.	errors	Yes
197	n.a.	n.a.	effort	Weak
197	n.a.	n.a.	design effort	Yes
208	Yes	No	effort	Yes
215	n.a.	n.a.	effort	No
216	Yes			

the metric if it was possible to demonstrate, in practice, that the metric was a strong predictor of factors that are associated with complexity. McCabe suggested this should include the effort required to test and maintain modules. As Table 3.2 indicates, the results of various empirical validation studies do not lend much credence to the metric. A more detailed account is given in Shepperd.[176] The clearest result is the strong relationship between cyclomatic complexity and LOC. Ironically, it was the 'inadequacy' of LOC as a module complexity metric that led McCabe to propose cyclomatic complexity as an alternative to the more traditional LOC.

The correlation with programming effort, although erratic, is not as damning as it appears on first sight. Testing is only a component of programming effort, and McCabe's original paper did not suggest that the metric be used as a predictor of software development effort. Instead, the objective was to create a measurement to provide an upper limit to module complexity. Thus, counting cyclomatic complexity across entire programs, rather than individual modules as some researchers have,[215] is not entirely appropriate. By contrast, the study by Basili and Perricone[12] deals with individual modules in which they examin possible associations between the error rate and module $v(G)$. One would expect the former to increase with the latter, presumably with a distinct step around the point of $v(G) = 10$.

Their results, however, suggest the complete reverse of this proposition and, although the result is counter-intuitive,* it throws considerable doubt upon $v(G)$ as a predictor of error-proneness. A more meaningful study would be to demonstrate that $v(G)$ is strongly correlated to testing effort, in particular unit testing, although, clearly, the actual testing strategy employed would have a considerable bearing upon the outcome of the investigation.

The small size of tasks being undertaken is another problem area. Both Woodward *et al.*[216] and Woodfield,[215, 214] use programs of less than 300 LOC, which, by software engineering standards, are trivial. In such situations the onus is upon the researcher to demonstrate that results on a small scale are equally applicable for large systems. Such a finding would be counter to current directions in software engineering.

$v(G)$ is sensitive to the number of sub-routines within a program, because McCabe suggests that these should be treated as unconnected components within the control graph. This has the bizarre result of increasing overall complexity as a program is divided into more, presumably simpler, modules.

In summary the limited work that has already been carried out is not very encouraging. The only convincing role for cyclomatic complexity is as an intra-modular complexity metric. Even this appears to have been rendered suspect by the work of Basili and Perricone. In any case, many researchers, for example Stevens *et al.*,[195] would argue that the problem of how to modularize a program is better resolved by considerations of inter-modular complexity.

It may well be that some find McCabe's metric 'intellectually very appealing',[216] but there are few grounds for its widespread adoption. Careful study of the empirical evidence shows erratic support for the measure, but a rather more consistent relationship with LOC. The likely explanation is that of cross-correlation. Decisions have a fairly constant incidence for a given application domain and development environment and, therefore, the cyclomatic number is almost certainly a proxy for size and so correlates with such metrics as LOC. The theoretical basis is equally insubstantial. The underlying model was not targeted by McCabe at any particular facet of program design and construction. Nor does it embody any notion of software structure — either at the intra-modular or inter-modular level.

One can only conclude that the utility of cyclomatic complexity as software metric is extremely restricted.†

---

*A possible explanation for this finding is that it is an artefact of using LOC for size normalization. A short module containing a single error will have a high error rate per unit length which can distort results if the overall number of errors relative to modules is not great.

†It might be argued that the metric would be useful in the context where one was interested in testing effort, and intended to apply some sort of path coverage strategy. Even this simple application has been disputed by Humphreys[86] due to the trade-off

FIG. 3.1. Local information flow from module A to module B.

3.4 Henry and Kafura's information flow measure

More recently, attention has focused on metrics derived from early in the software life-cycle. The metric that has excited the most attention is the design measure proposed by Sallie Henry and Denis Kafura,[81, 82, 83] known as the information flow metric. It is widely considered to be the classic design metric, being more widely cited and investigated than any other design metric.

The basic idea behind Kafura and Henry's work is that of information flow which is based upon the concept that the complexity of a software module — a functional design unit — is related to the number flows or channels of information between it and its environment. In addition, a module has an internal complexity which, they suggested, might be based on module size and measured as LOC. Thus, the model incorporates the concept of internal and external module complexity, although in practice most attention has been given to external complexity. Such ideas are loosely derived from the design evaluation criteria of module coupling and cohesion described by Stevens *et al.*[195] The calculation of the metric is as follows.

Connections are defined as channels or information flows whereby one module can influence another. The following types of information flow are defined, where in each case there is a flow from module A to module B:

- local flows which may either be direct when module A passes parameters to B (Figure 3.1), or indirect when A returns a value to B (Figure 3.1), or module C calls A and B and passes the result value from A to B (Figure 3.2);
- global flows where module A writes to a data structure DS and B reads from DS (Figure 3.2).

A module's connections to its environment are a function of its fan-in and fan-out. The fan-in fi of a procedure is the number of local flows that terminate at that procedure, plus the number of data structures from which

between decision complexity and data structure complexity, as exemplified by the use of decision tables.

FIG. 3.2. Indirect local information flow from module A to module B, via
C and via DS.

information is retrieved. The fan-out fo is the number of local flows that
originate from a procedure, plus the number of data structures updated.
The total number of input to output path combinations per procedure is
given by:

$$(fi * fi) \tag{3.12}$$

This is given a weighting by raising it to the power of two in order to reflect
the belief of Kafura and Henry that connective complexity is a non-linear
function:

$$(fi * fo)^2 \tag{3.13}$$

This complexity is combined with the internal complexity of the procedure,
measured by LOC, to give a measure of procedure complexity as:

$$length * (fi * fo)^2 \tag{3.14}$$

A multiplicative relationship was adopted in Equation 3.13 between internal and connective complexity, as the two were considered to be orthogonal
and also because it indicated the number of potential information flow paths
through the module.

A number of applications have been suggested for the information flow
metric. It may be used to identify potential problem modules by concentrating upon outliers (i.e. those with abnormally high complexities). This
technique has been used with some success in a recent type of case study
validation.[104] Another application described by the Henry and Kafura in
their original study of the UNIX operating system[83] is the analysis of metric
trends between levels in a calling hierarchy of procedures. A sharp increase
in complexity between levels indicates design problems, possibly a missing
level of abstraction.

The type of problem that a designer might hope to identify include:

- lack of cohesion (i.e. more than one function);
- stress points where there is a high level of 'through traffic';
- inadequate refinement (e.g. a missing level of abstraction);

Table 3.3 *Empirical validations of information flow*

Study	Attribute	Better than LOC?	Correlated with LOC?	Correlated with resource?	Better with length?
82	Changes	Yes	No	Yes	No
102	Coding time +errors	No	n.a.	Yes	Yes
104	Maintainability	Equal	Yes	Yes	n.a.
164	Modifiability	No	n.a.	No	Yes
164	Maintainability	Yes	n.a.	Yes	Yes
164	Comprehension	Yes	n.a.	Yes	Yes
164	Locality	Yes	n.a.	Yes	No
112	Errors	No	Weak	Weak	n.a.
179	Devmnt. effort	Yes	Weak	No	No
180	Maintainability	No	Yes	Yes	Yes

- overloaded data structures where there is a need to segment.

Henry and Kafura have applied their metric to the UNIX operating system, and have had some success in identifying problem areas. They also found a high correlation ($r = 0.95$) between information flow and number of errors — measured as the number of program changes.[84] Interestingly, they found that the procedure length component of the metric actually detracted from its performance, and that a Spearman correlation of $r = 0.98$ was obtained without the inclusion of length in the metric. As has already been stated, the information flow metric is unusual in that it has been the subject of a number of empirical investigations. These are summarized in Table 3.3.

It is apparent that the studies are varied in nature and have produced results that are rather mixed. This is in part due to Henry and Kafura's approach. Just as for the other metrics previously discussed, their basic model does not indicate those aspects of software or the software process that are being addressed, leaving, as a default, a degree of universalism that may not be fully warranted. In their original work,[81, 82] the metric is used to predict the number of changes per procedure within the UNIX operating system. These are treated as a proxy for error data.* However, the motivation for the work is variously reported as the high cost of software maintenance,[82] the high cost of software development,[81] improving software reliability,[83] providing quantitative guidelines for the software designer,[84] and controlling software complexity.[81] Nowhere is this confu-

---

*Henry and Kafura argue that this is a legitimate assumption, citing the work of Dunsmore and Gannon[50] and Basili and Reiter[14] as precedents, although in her doctoral dissertation Henry does concede that the 'suggested changes to UNIX consist of both actual errors and some necessary performance enhancements'.[81]

Table 3.4 *Data from the UNIX study*

Order of complexity	No. of procedures	No. of 'error' procedures	%
0	17	2	12
1	38	12	32
2	41	19	46
3	27	19	70
4	26	15	58
5	12	11	92
6	3	2	67
7	1	0	0
Totals	165	80	

sion more evident than in the statement of the problem in Sallie Henry's doctoral dissertation:[81]

> The thesis of this research is that a set of measurements based on the flow of information connecting system components can be used to evaluate software design and implementation.

The 64 000 dollar question — evaluate with respect to what — has apparently been overlooked. Such oversights are all too typical of the 'software complexity syndrome'. The various interpretations given by different researchers to the model are thus not surprising. We now review the empirical evidence in more detail. The empirical work, cited by Henry and Kafura to support the metric, is based upon a change analysis of parts of the UNIX operating system. Very high correlations are reported, for example Spearman $r = 0.94$, $p = 0.0214$ [82] and Pearson's product moment* $r = 0.95$ [84] between the metric and module changes.† A matter of slight concern is their discovery that information flow is out-performed by McCabe's cyclomatic complexity metric.[84‡] Given our previous discussion linking Mc-Cabe's measure to LOC, this suggests that a simple size measure is as good or better predictor of software changes. Closer inspection, however, raises a number of question marks over the entire empirical study.

Table 3.4, which uses logarithmic class interval analysis is taken from Henry's doctoral thesis.[81] This reveals that of the 165 UNIX procedures examined, 80 were modified or, as Henry would have it, contained errors.

---

*This is in actual fact an inappropriate test, given that the assumption of normally distributed data points is scarcely credible for change or error data.

† Henry and Kafura rather misleadingly refer to change data as 'error data' on a number of occasions, see, for example, Henry, Kafura and Harris.[84] A model of maintenance work is unlikely to be isomorphic to a reliability model.

‡ To complete a picture of confusion, Kafura gives different correlation coefficients for the same study.[103] Reference back to Henry's original thesis[81] suggests that the Kafura paper contains typographical errors.

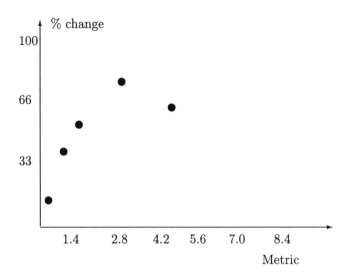

FIG. 3.3. Percentage of procedures changed vs. information flow metric.

Elsewhere,[81] Henry states that a total of 80 changes was analysed. Presumably the explanation for there being exactly one change per changed procedure lies in the counting method, so that no account is given of the size of a change and the analysis covers only one UNIX update. If this is not the case, one can only comment that it is very remarkable that no procedure is subject to more than one change.

The choice of logarithmic class interval analysis used by Henry is a surprising one. First, one loses a lot of data, particularly from the higher-order classes, resulting in what is at best a weak ordering. Second, it decreases the number of data points from 165 to 8, making statistical significance more difficult to obtain and trends less reliable. Unfortunately, insufficient data is provided to perform an alternative analysis, though we feel compelled to point out that on the basis of the above data we obtain a Spearman correlation coefficient of 0.21 and not 0.94. Figure 3.3 shows the distribution of data points as a scatter diagram. The difference is presumably due to Henry and Kafura eliminating the upper two class intervals from their analysis, the justification being that there are insufficient procedures within these classes,[82] and that the procedures are too complex to be changed.[81, 82] Thus their major result rests on a correlation of just six data points in rank ordering.

The other major result that Henry and Kafura present is that the length, or the internal module complexity component of their metric actually detracts from its overall performance.[82] Without length and using class intervals based on $10^{n/2}$, a Spearman correlation of $r = 0.98$ was obtained.

No justification is proffered for what appear to be rather arbitrary class intervals, which is rather disappointing given their material bearing upon this style of analysis.

These results suggest that the information flow metric has identified some relationship between design or system architecture and software reliability, but that it is less compelling than might appear at first sight. If one were to summarize the remainder of the results given in Table 3.3 it would be to support the view that underlying the metric is a powerful idea, but considerably more work in verification and refinement is required.

Three out of the six remaining investigations find useful — from a software engineering perspective — relationships between the metric and a variety of software quality factors. A fourth study[164] indicates that for three out of four maintenance factors the metric proved to be an effective indicator. Kitchenham[112] found only weak relationships and superior performance using more traditional code-based metrics. A sixth study[179] found no statistically valid relationship with either information flow or executable LOC and development effort, although the design metric performed marginally better. The table is weakly suggestive of some association with LOC[104, 112, 179, 180] and ambiguous as to the efficacy of including LOC into the formulation of the metric. Two studies[82, 179] suggest that this detracts from performance, but Rombach[164] finds in most cases that it enhances performance, as does the Kafura and Reddy case study.[104] It is fortunate that the module length component of their metric is of marginal significance, as otherwise this would diminish the ability to use information flow at design time.

One of the difficulties confronting those wishing to validate the information flow metric empirically stems from the inadequate and conflicting definitions that Henry and Kafura give, particularly concerning indirect flows. Again, as with the other two metrics, informality predominates. For example, what is a global data structure? What is a procedure? The definitions of information flow used in calculating the metric are ambiguous and capricious.

A major source of anomaly are the many local indirect flows that may only be detected by internal analysis of a module. This is shown in Figure 3.4. Unfortunately, such information is unlikely to be available during the system design stage of software development. Even if one obtained the necessary data, a static analysis would be inadequate, as the existence of the flow is entirely dependent upon the execution order of the code. Dynamic analysis, apart from being a difficult enterprise, generates results that reflect the input chosen to exercise the code. There are no obvious guidelines to steer the would-be software metrologist as to the choice of input. However, to fail to capture indirect flows-by-assignment leaves the measure vulnerable to the whimsy of the software designer in his or her choice of data object name.

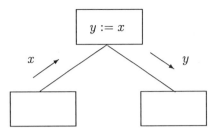

FIG. 3.4. Indirect local flows 'hidden' at design time.

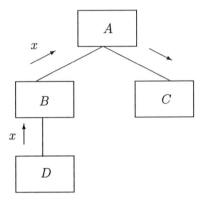

FIG. 3.5. Indirect local flow across more than two levels.

The definition of local indirect flows as given by Kafura and Henry,[103] would appear to encompass flow over only two levels of a system structure. If such flows are to be counted, there is no good reason why the number of levels should be restricted to two. For instance, Figure 3.5 shows an indirect local flow which has a scope of three levels.

However, simply extending the number of levels included is unsatisfactory, since the outcome is potential overcounting, particularly if the problems over indirect flow-by-assignment, described above, are addressed. The consequence is that all modules are linked to all other modules, except where a system comprises entirely independent modules that could run in a completely unconstrained fashion, in an arbitrary order. Such systems are unlikely to be useful and, given their very special nature, it seems likely that they would be amenable to an entirely separate family of metrics and models. Therefore, one must have grave reservations concerning

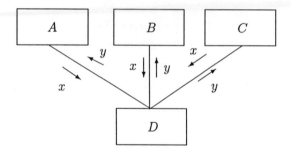

FIG. 3.6. Information flow and module reuse.

the validity of indirect flows.* These reservations are reinforced by the fact that indirect flows do not seem to correspond to any obvious 'real world' design process or entity.[91] The equation for the metric is poorly formulated in that a single zero term is propagated through to result in an overall measure of zero. This is possible even if the module has, say, a large fan-out and comprises many LOC. It would seem that Henry and Kafura circumvented this problem in their original analysis by ignoring what they termed 'memoryless procedures' on the basis that to do otherwise would mean that 'connections between procedures would be generated that do not functionally exist.'[81] In fact, the problem that Henry and Kafura are trying to avoid is the problem of module reuse. In other words, the separate instantiations of a reused module should not be a vehicle for information flow transmission. Unfortunately, they seem to have adopted a solution leading to three problems. First, the fact that a module is memoryless does not mean ordinarily that there is no interest in its behaviour. Second, potentially complex components, but with either a zero fan-in or fan-out, are invariably identified as having the minimum level of errors (presumably

Table 3.5 *Comparison of module reuse and duplication*

Module	With reuse			With duplication		
	Fin	Fout	Complexity	Fin	Fout	Complexity
A	1	1	1	1	1	1
B	1	1	1	1	1	1
C	1	1	1	1	1	1
D	3	3	81	1	1	1
E				1	1	1
F				1	1	1
Total			84			6

*Kitchenham takes a similar view in her decision to omit such flows from her empirical investigation of design metrics.[112]

zero), or whatever quality is being analysed. Third, the serious problem of module reuse leads to specious information flows being counted. As the model stands it penalizes the reuse of any module that exports or imports any information, due to its quadratic nature. Such an example is given in Figure 3.6 and Table 3.5. The terms *Fin* and *Fout* in Table 3.5 refer to fan-in and fan-out.

Such problems are disconcerting in that they lead to the metric being difficult to apply and analyse[89] and must, in part, explain the extent to which empirical results differ, as, clearly, module reuse levels will vary between different environments.

A more rigorous analysis of the metric equations reveals anomalies in the treatment of parameterized communication as compared with communication via global data structures. Despite defining global information flows (those via global data structures), Henry and Kafura fail to incorporate them into their definition of fan-in and fan-out. Instead, they merely use a count of data structure accesses. Potentially, this has a considerable impact upon their measure, as illustrated in Figure 3.7 and Table 3.6. Counting reads and writes, as opposed to global flows, becomes significant when more than two modules communicate via a global data structure.[91]

Another ground for criticism of information flow as a metric is that the model makes extremely simplistic assumptions concerning the nature of the information. All flows are considered to have uniform complexity, but the information might be a simple boolean or a complex structure containing many record variants — the metric is not sensitive to the difference. Thus, complex connections between modules could be disguised and not captured as information flows.   Moreover, as discussed previously in connection with the empirical evidence, the use of length as a measure of intra-modular complexity is debatable. Its late availability is also a problem if information flow is to be used as a true design metric. Henry and Kafura raise the possibility of refining this measure by replacing it with either Halstead's E measure or McCabe's cyclomatic complexity.[83] However,

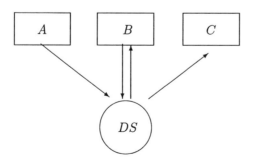

FIG. 3.7. Information flow mechanisms.

Table 3.6 *Comparison of the treatment of global flows*

Module	Accesses counted		Global flows counted	
	Fan-in	Fan-out	Fan-in	Fan-out
A	0	1	0	2
B	1	1	1	1
C	1	0	2	0

given the problems that are inherent in both of these metrics it is doubtful whether this would represent much of an improvement. Further, their use would also delay the availability of the metric.

The would-be-investigator is also confounded by the absence of definitions. In particular, global data structures and parameters remain undefined. Certainly, in many environments, there would seem to be good grounds for treating devices as global data structures. Whether this should be extended to include screen output — and even keyboard input — are moot points. What is clear, though, is the paucity of Henry and Kafura's underlying model in these respects.

Kitchenham also criticizes the metric as an example of a 'synthetic',[112] in that it combines disparate primitive counts, thus leading to potential confusion and difficulty in application. There is no doubt that it has confused and obscured notions of information and procedural flow and it is arguable that these are best kept distinct so as to facilitate the diagnosis of the underlying causes of any symptoms detected by the information flow metric.

In conclusion, there are two main problems with Henry and Kafura's information flow metric. The authors have no clear idea of what they are modelling, and seem to commute between a variety of problem domains, almost as if they are interchangeable. Until goals for the metric are clearly stated it will be severely hampered in its application. The other problem is one of approach. Having adopted what appears to be a plausible idea, and one consistent with current thinking in software engineering, they have proceeded to obscure it under a facade of informality and arbitrariness. Many of the inconsistencies and anomalies contained within their model could have been avoided had a more formal approach been adopted.

3.5   Unfulfilled promises

What can we conclude from our dissection of the three most influential software metrics of the past 20 years? Is the fact that none of them appear satisfactory ill chance? If only the metrologists had chosen different numbers would all have been different? In the authors' opinion, to be so seriously in error three times is not mere bad luck but carelessness;

it suggests that current approaches adopted towards software metrics are inappropriate.

It should be stressed, however, that it is not the individual factors being measured that are being criticized, but, rather, the approach to the application and interpretation of software measurement. This chapter and, to a lesser extent, Chapter 2, have revealed a recurring pattern of ill-conceived and poorly articulated models that underlie the metrics presented above. This, in turn, has led to metrics that are anomalous and out of step with current developments in software engineering. Despite the fundamental nature of these problems, they have all too often been obscured due to the lowly role ascribed to the model. Directly stemming from modelling weaknesses are the problems of empirical validation. Empirical validation of a software metric is quite difficult enough, without being uncertain as to what is being validated.

In short, the problems of software metrics are those of foundation and methodology. And this is the starting point for the research described in this book. It is evident from the survey of metrics research described in the last two chapters that the general tenor of the work has been a preoccupation with detail, arguably at the expense of higher-level issues such as what does the metric mean, how might it be evaluated and, finally, how might it be integrated into the software engineering process? Each of these topics will be reviewed briefly.

- The first issue is, what does a metric mean? The reader will have noticed copious references to models and underlying models in the preceding chapters because it is only within the context of a model or a theory that a measurement has a meaning.[119] Consider the measurement observation that a piece of code has a luminosity of x. This cannot be interpreted because there is no theory or model to link the measurement with any other software engineering property of code — at least as far as the authors are aware, apart from a slight suspicion that day-glo code might be injurious to one's eyesight! We cannot say whether a luminosity of x is good or bad. Nor can it be stated whether it will lead to problems of reliability, and so on and so forth. Evidently, this is an extreme example, but, equally, it should be clear that the metrics that have been reviewed have all relied upon implicit ideas, unspoken assumptions, and partial definitions in terms of their underlying models. Consequently, there is a need for the development of a more formal framework for software metric models.

- The second issue is model evaluation. Since, in many respects, a model may be thought of as a theory, then it is natural that we should wish to evaluate the theory; this might be accomplished by means of empirical methods — for example through experimentation — or by more formal techniques, such as the application of axioms and proofs.

It has been a major theme of this and the preceding chapter that scant regard has been paid to model evaluation. To some extent this has been inevitable, given the informal approach to modelling adopted by the majority of researchers, but it is also the consequence of *ad hoc* ideas and the absence of any systematic method for tackling the problem of model evaluation. The importance of validation cannot be overstressed, since metrics based upon flawed models are worse than valueless: they are potentially misleading. This book seeks to remedy this deficiency by describing the development of a coherent infrastructure for the validation of software models.

- The third issue is the clear need for some method to guide software engineers in the selection and tailoring of software metrics to be suitable for their particular measurement goals. A major criticism of much past work has been the unfounded belief in 'General Complexity Metrics' of one form or another, which are suitable for all problems in almost any environment. This has led to the view that metric selection is something akin to an 'off-the-shelf' process. The search for some alternative approach yields two benefits. First, it raises the level of concern above the current obsession with metric minutiae that bedevils so much current work; and, second, it forces more careful definition of measurement goals, with the attendant reduction in evaluation difficulties. If it is unclear what is being measured it is not easy to know if it is being done effectively!

These three issues, then, will be addressed in the remainder of this book.

4

MODELS, THEORIES, AND METRICS

Synopsis

The preceding two chapters have described major problems that afflict the software metrics area. These can be directly ascribed to inadequate theories and a lack of attention to the modelling process. This chapter first examines the main concepts of measurement theory; looks at the relationship between measurement and modelling; and then describes the difficult subject of model evaluation. It concludes with an examination of some of the attempts to remedy problems in software metrication based on measurement theory and axiomatic descriptions. They are found wanting.

4.1 Introduction

The analysis of developments in software metrics in the two preceding chapters suggests that measurement is understood and applied on a very informal basis. In particular, Chapters 2 and 3 have demonstrated that software metrologists have a rather weak notion of modelling which, as a consequence, has profound implications upon progress within the whole subject area. The justification for the use of metrics as an adjunct to software development has tended to run along the following lines.[47]

> You can't control what you can't measure. In most disciplines, the strong linkage between measurement and control is taken for granted.

Other engineering disciplines are able to take and utilize measurements in order to provide quality control, and even more alluring, accurate predictions. Software engineering does not compare favourably with other engineering disciplines. *Ergo*, we should make greater use of software measurements, which will result in cheaper, more reliable, and useful software products.

Thus far it would be difficult to disagree, but the corollary that many infer: that almost any measurement renders the software engineer better off is highly debatable; that a measurement, even if it is not directly useful, will cause the software engineer to regard the software product in a more analytical fashion and, by some mysterious inductive process, that it will yield greater insights. Such an analysis fails to understand the nature of measurement in other more mature disciplines. It is perhaps instructive to examine the measurement of temperature, which is a well understood and tolerably reliable process, prior to describing attempts at addressing the problems that were described in the preceding two chapters.

One of the interesting features about temperature measurement is that it is not, in general, measured directly. The most common approach is to measure length: length of a column of mercury contained in a thermometer. This is an example of indirect measurement. It is not that temperature cannot be measured directly,[119] but, rather, that it is more convenient and accurate to do so indirectly.

How is it, then, that we can satisfy ourselves that there exists a reliable relationship between the length of a column of mercury and temperature? It is possible that we might start with the supposition of some theoretical relationship (e.g. a linear function) between the indirect measurement and actual temperature. Empirical observation and experimentation is then required to confirm or refute the relationship. Alternatively, our starting point may be drawn from the observation that mercury expands with increases in temperature, and this may then be formalized into a set of equations.

Careful observation of our thermometer in a wide range of environments reveals that what appeared to be a simple linear relationship between length of mercury and temperature is, in fact, somewhat more complex. For instance, it is particularly evident that the thermometer fails to perform accurately on the top of Mount Everest. Also, mercury thermometers are restricted by the fact that mercury will vaporize at high temperatures and, therefore, cannot measure temperatures much over 350 degrees Centigrade. Thus, the measurement of temperature by thermometer is dependent upon a number of factors and is subject to certain limitations.

In practice one can compensate for temperature readings at different altitudes since we can make the model more sophisticated as we begin to understand the problem domain better. So, we model the way in which temperature, altitude, and pressure are related in a systematic way. Thus, more than one factor is required. The perception of temperature as part of a system is an example of a major development in our ability to measure accurately.

The final point to draw from this brief peroration into thermometry is the problem of error. The quantitative/qualitative or objective/subjective dichotomy is, in at least one sense, misleading because, in practice, one is confronted by a continuum. Some measurement practices, such as thermometer measurement of temperature, are more repeatable than others, for example the measurement of aesthetics. The term *repeatable* is meant in the sense of a low frequency of errors, small error size, and a normally distributed set of errors.

Let us now return to program development and software engineering. The remainder of this chapter examines the issues raised by the foregoing discussion in more depth, namely: the different types of measurement and their characteristics; the conditions that must hold true for each type of measurement; the relationship between model and metric; and the issue of measurement reliability. We then examine two attempts at putting metrication on a firmer theoretical basis.

4.2   The theory of measurement

At this rather belated stage it is appropriate to consider more exactly what is meant by measurement. Using Pfanzagl's definition,[154] measurement is taken to be the process of assigning numbers* to describe some empirical attribute of a product or event by rule. The rules that govern the number assignment are fundamental since they introduce varying degrees of objectivity into the process. None the less the boundary between measurement and non-measurement is a fuzzy one.

In this section we review classical measurement theory briefly and discuss the extent to which it does, and ought to, impinge upon current practice in the software metrics field.

4.2.1   *Types of measurement*

As the example of temperature measurement has revealed, measurement may be one of two types: direct or indirect. Indirect measurement occurs whenever one or more other entities are measured in order to provide a measure of an object or event of interest. Direct measurement occurs if no other measurements are required. Within the domain of software metrics, indirect measurements are most commonplace. Indirect measurement is usually employed for the reason that temporal considerations prevent direct measurement because the measurement is being used in a predictive capacity. This has an important implication, in that a phenomenological link is required to relate the indirect measure, or measures, to the object of the measurement process.

4.2.2   *Scales for measurement*

Classical measurement literature identifies the following four types of measurement scale:†

---

*On occasions one might assign other mathematical entities instead of numbers,[118] for instance vectors as in the case of the Myers'[143] extension to the cyclomatic number metric. To do so is, however, rarely judicious, as this leads to deep methodological problems given the absence of any generally plausible greater-than or less-than relations and, as a sequitur, little theoretical basis for anything other than a nominal scale. Another example of non-numeric measurement is the case of nominal scales where the numbers merely serve as labels and can therefore be legitimately substituted by letters or any other unique identifier.

†To be more exact, there is a non-denumerable infinity of scales, including such exotica as the logarithmic interval scale[193] and the hyperordinal scale;[199] these, however, have no, or only marginal, empirical application.

Table 4.1 *Properties of measurement scales*

Scale	Basic empirical operations	Mathematical group structure
Nominal	=	permutation group $M' = f(M)$
Ordinal	=,<,>	isotonic group $M' = f(M)$ where $f(M)$ is any monotonic increasing function
Interval	=,<,>, equality of intervals	general linear group $M' = \alpha M + \beta,\ \alpha > 0$
Ratio	=,<,>, equality of intervals and ratios	similarity group $M' = \alpha M,$ $\alpha > 0$

- *Nominal scale*, for example the numbering of football players.
- *Ordinal scale*, for example the hardness of minerals.
- *Interval scale*, for example temperature in degrees Centigrade.
- *Ratio scale*, for example temperature on the Kelvin scale or length.

Naturally, each scale has different properties or empirical operations associated with it, and is required to satisfy different axioms. These are given in Table 4.1, adapted from Stevens.[193] Let us review each scale in turn. The nominal scale is the least restricted, and therefore the simplest of all the measurement scales. The only empirical operation that is required for this form of measurement is the determination of equality — by which we mean empirical indistinguishability. This binary relation is reflexive, symmetric, and transitive. Examples of nominal measurement are the much cited case of football player numbers and, within the area of software engineering, the classification of software systems by the basic COCOMO model[24] as organic, semi- detached or embedded. It is noteworthy that in the latter case no use is made of numerals. However, the assignment process is still carried out according to rules, even if these are only informally stated; hence it may be considered a process of measurement.

The ordinal scale introduces rank ordering, derived from the empirical weak ordering relations, less-than and greater-than. These relations are reflexive and transitive. Again, COCOMO[24] can be used to provide examples, this time from the intermediate model, where cost drivers — for example, the size of the database — are placed on a scale ranging from very-low to extra-high. Although, we may determine empirically that a very-low sized database is less than an extra-high database, it is not possible to assert anything concerning the size of the difference. While this is fairly self-evident for the above example, were we to substitute numerals for the names of the classes, for example to rate database size from 1 to 5, it might be more tempting to succumb to such a temptation. For similar reasons, one must exercise caution concerning the application of statistics to ordinal or, for that matter, nominal scales.[192, 193]

The possibility of comparing measurement intervals empirically introduces the interval scale, a scale that is quantitative in the normal meaning of the word, excepting a defined absolute zero. The most commonplace example is temperature measurement using degrees Centigrade. Since zero degrees is arbitrarily placed, it is not possible to state that 10 degrees Centigrade is twice as hot as 5 degrees Centigrade, although it is empirically possible to determine that the difference between 10 degrees and 5 degrees is the same as the difference between 20 degrees and 15 degrees.

Ratio scales differ from interval scales in that absolute zero is always implied — as in temperature measurement by the Kelvin scale. Consequently, it is possible to determine equality of ratios in addition to equality of intervals. Software metrics offer many such examples, ranging from LOC to Halstead's E metric.

In many cases it is obvious from the empirical operations available to us, what scale we are dealing with. More formal mechanisms for the determination of scale type do, however, exist. These are based upon transformations that are possible upon the measurement group structure* which still preserve empirical orderings.[63, 192, 193, 199] Nominal scales may undergo transformation by any one-to-one function, due to the absence of even weak ordering. By contrast, the only permissible class of transformation for a ratio scale is of the form $M = \alpha M$ for non-negative values of α. Table 4.1 lists all permissible transformations for each scale type.

The final point to make while examining scale types is the extent to which ratio measurement is in some sense 'better' than nominal or ordinal measurement. Adams[1] argues that by merely viewing measurement in terms of the axioms or conditions necessary for a certain scale of measurement to be possible, one can lose sight of purpose. He gives the example of mineral measurement using Moh's hardness scale (ordinal), which is wholly adequate for the purpose of mineral identification in the field, not an unfortunate necessity imposed by the difficulty of establishing the conditions necessary for interval or ratio measurement.

What significance does the foregoing discussion have for software metrology? The answer is threefold:

- The distinction between direct and indirect measurement is an important one. Indirect measurement, while being widely used within the field of software metrics, places an additional burden upon the

---

*By structure we mean the relational structure $< N, R >$ where N is the set of all numbers (or observations for an empirical structure) and R is the set of all relations. For an ordinal scale the measurement structure is therefore $< N, \geq >$, for a ratio scale it would be $< N, \geq, + >$.

researcher — *viz* the need to justify the theory linking the indirect to the direct measure.

- The type of scale may restrict meaningful statistical manipulation and observation. A common problem arises when one wishes to establish a statistical mean over an ordinal-type measurement, since to do so requires the assumption of constant intervals between all the points on the scale. Should such a situation prevail, the scale would be an interval scale or possibly a ratio scale.

- The identification of scale type introduces certain axioms that must be satisfied by a theoretical analysis of the metric and its underlying model. In brief, it is necessary to show that two theorems hold for the measurement: the Representation Theorem and the Uniqueness Theorem.[118, 199]

The second point is one that is often missed by metrics researchers. For example, the Henry and Kafura information flow metric[82] provides an interesting application of empirical meaningfulness being restricted by scale. The metric is an example of an indirect measure of software complexity based upon counts of information flows between modules. As a direct measure — treated merely as simple counts — the information flows must be placed on a ratio scale.*

However, the part of their model which relates an indirect measure to the quantity of interest, software complexity, is the term

$$(fi * fo)^2 \qquad\qquad (4.1)$$

where fi is the fan-in and fo is the fan-out of modules. The quadratic nature causes it to behave as a monotonically increasing function.† This transformation is weak order preserving — but no more. As a consequence the only meaningful remarks that may be made concerning this metric are those that are based upon the relations of equivalence and weak ordering. For example, it would not be admissable to state that module x with a value of 100 is twice as complex as module y with a value of 50. Observations of interval size or ratio have no empirical meaning.‡

The Representation Theorem requires that the numbers assigned by the measurement process must represent observed empirical relations properly. In order for this to be the case there must be a homomorphic or isomorphic

---

*This is because the only transformation that does not lead to loss of ordering information is of the form $M = \alpha M$.

†The function is monotonically increasing because the information flow counts and the fan-in and fan-out must be non-negative.

‡Though, in general, meaningless statements should be avoided, occasionally pragmatic considerations may overrule. Finkelstein and Leaning[63] give the example of using the arithmetic mean, rather than the median, of a set of examination marks despite being measured in an ordinal fashion.

mapping from the empirical to the chosen number system.* Unfortunately, this theorem is less useful in practice than one might suppose, since for any finite or denumerable empirical system there can always be found some numeric system that is isomorphic to it,[199] though this may be by virtue of employing 'unnatural or pathological' relations. Worse still, there may be little agreement about the empirical relations, because, for instance, we may not all agree that program x is more complex than y. Consequently, paying attention to this theorem is only a minor aspect of metric evaluation. By itself, it is insufficient. The effort of formal proof is therefore seldom justified; rather, informal reasoning is adequate to check for 'gross' errors.†

The discussion of scales has already touched upon aspects of the Uniqueness Theorem. Measurement is unique up to certain levels of transformation so, for example, non-Kelvin temperature measurement may be multiplied by or added to a constant (or both) without loss of uniqueness for the type of scale adopted. Satisfaction of this theorem, therefore, is concerned with the formal proof that all numerical relations are equivalent to all empirical relations for all permissible mappings from the empirical system on to the numerical or measurement system. This is a formalization of our earlier discussion of suitable scales.

Although compliance with these theorems is a necessary step in the theoretical validation of a metric — a point that will be taken up again later in the book — they are not a panacea for software measurement. Fundamental difficulties remain, in particular, errors in the modelling process and the measuring process.

Clearly, there is no simple redress for erroneous modelling of software,‡ since it is the outcome of our current lack of understanding about software engineering processes and their interaction with products. However, the theory described thus far is idealistic, in that it incorporates no notion of uncertainty in obtaining measurements or empirical relations. Such a theory will also require a profound understanding and models of the software development process.

Two possible solutions to errors in the measuring process are the application of a statistical theory of errors coupled with a linguistic framework

---

*As we have already noted, measurement need not be limited to the assignment of numbers. In such circumstances the establishment of a homomorphism can be an involved process, although extremely important, since the properties of the measuring system will be less well understood than the familiar number system.

†This conclusion would be strongly disputed by other researchers such as Kaposi and Myers.[105] However, in the end the problem reduces to one's views of the empirical world, and the need to find mappings between this world and the closed system of classical measurement theory.

‡Obviously there is a blurred distinction between model and measurement error, to the extent that the former will lead to the latter. Whether this is amenable to statistical remedy depends largely upon the size of the scatter and the nature of the distribution.

to describe reports (observations),[119] and an extension of the formal machinery in order to axiomatize uncertainty, for example semi-orders.[130] The former approach is more promising in that it attempts to use statistical means to establish a link from the uncertain empirical world to an ideal world of absolute certainty. The latter approach provides no such mechanism. In a sense, formality and closure imply an inevitable retreat from the 'real world'.

The conclusion must be that software metrologists ought to be aware of classical measurement theory and the restrictions that it imposes for meaningful measurement. In addition, it should be equally clear that the majority of hard problems remain unaddressed by measurement theory, the chief of these being errors in modelling and measurement.

4.3   Modelling and measurement

4.3.1   *Measurement and purpose*

Having introduced the idea that measurement requires a model to permit meaningful application and evaluation, it is worth examining the concept a little more carefully. A model is an abstraction or simplification of reality. Thus, the first concern when a model is developed is that it serves some stated purpose. Without a purpose we cannot know which aspects of the real world to incorporate and which to exclude during model development. Modelling in a vacuum is a rather curious endeavour. It is, however, a potential pitfall for academics who may not be immediately confronted by a problem. The research of such academics can easily degenerate into rather an aimless activity — *vide* Bache and Tinker[7] for an example of a mathematically rigorous model, but one which unfortunately happens to be almost orthogonal to the objectives of the research which are variously stated as measuring 'cognitive complexity', 'bugs', and 'number of changes'. While we would wish to applaud their desire to introduce a little more formality into the world of software metrics, the conclusion that we have reached is that the model, rather than the problem, has become pre-eminent in the minds of the researchers. Similar charges could be levelled at the early work of Fenton *et al.*,[61, 59, 60, 57, 58] where the problem domain appears to be of little importance relative to the development of a formal model.

A model will establish relationships between various entities. In order to explain this, consider modelling the consumption of printer paper in a software development company. We postulate a relationship between Source lines of code (SLOC) and the quantity of paper required. It is often helpful to express these relationships more precisely as equations. In doing so this encourages rigorous thinking and a better understanding of the problem domain. It also facilitates validation. Developing the stationery example, we might more formally specify the model as:

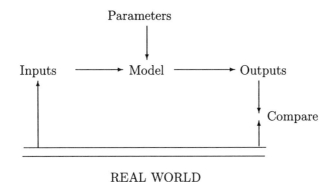

FIG. 4.1. The relationship between a model and 'reality'

$$cns = f(SLOC) \qquad (4.2)$$

where cns is the paper consumption. This immediately raises issues of how we relate our abstract model to the real world. What is consumption of paper? What units do we propose to use? Is there a time dimension to consumption? To keep matters simple let us suppose that the answer to the last question is no. As for units, the page seems a reasonable candidate. This now gives some clues for the function f which will be the reciprocal of the number of lines per page giving:

$$cns = SLOC/n \qquad (4.3)$$

where n is the number of lines that may be printed per page. To generalize, a model will have inputs and outputs, sometimes known as endogenous and exogenous variables. These are linked by relationships, or by a set of equalities which may use parameters, as in the example above where n allows the model to be used for a variety of printers and stationery sizes. This is illustrated in Figure 4.1.

A model should also define the mapping from the real world on to the inputs and outputs identified. This establishes the essential two-way link between abstract space and reality. There is the measurement process (effectively a mapping from the real world onto the model) and the prediction process (a mapping from the model back on to the real world). When no such connections exist the model is metaphysical.

It is immediately clear that this framework is not made explicit in any of the metrics discussed in preceding chapters. Difficulties with unspecified or ambiguous mappings have manifested themselves as counting problems and as the prediction of metaphysical properties. Perhaps the latter is the most disturbing issue in that metrics are being used to predict metaphysical properties, most frequently complexity. When we are faced with definitions, even those intended to be ironical, such as 'a not-so-warm feeling in the tummy',[41] this must be treated as a warning sign.

Developing the notion of the metaphysical further, we would like to make a rather contentious proposition:

> Not all software properties are measurable or even directly observable, in any useful engineering sense.

Recall that measurement implies the existence of rules for the assignment of numbers, labels, vectors, etc. Where the rules are unknown or non-existent we do not consider this to be measurement and the property is metaphysical. For example, 'user-friendliness' cannot be measured as such, unless the rules for this task are defined. This does not preclude informal rule definition.*

However, we consider informal rule definition to be somewhat specious, as 'user-friendliness' is sufficiently nebulous to make operational definition difficult. If it cannot be defined, then the rules for assigning numbers cannot be defined, and no intelligible measurement is possible. Nor can it be claimed to be measured indirectly, as there is no way of establishing the validity of the hypothesis linking the indirect measurement to 'user-friendliness' because of the problems of establishing an empirical relationship between the indirect and our undefinable measure.† Instead, we must conclude that 'user-friendliness' has something of a metaphysical flavour about it. Metaphysical properties can be of immense importance and interest; however, to set out to measure something that is fundamentally

---

*In practice, we attempt to measure some of the possible consequences of 'user-friendliness', or the lack of it, by employing an indirect measuring technique. We may choose to measure the time taken by a user to perform a particular task and hypothesize that the results have a particular significance; thus, we have measured 'user-friendliness' indirectly in a manner analogous to the measurement of temperature by the vertical height of a column of mercury.

†This argument could be construed as a rather intoxicating concoction of Popperian empirical refutation and Bridgman's doctrine of operationalism. Both ingredients are potentially troublesome. Empirical refutation, taken to its logical conclusion, argues that only the metaphysical may be regarded as irrefutable, a position that could be somewhat inconvenient for the software metrologist as it may not be desirable to call into question the fundamental axioms of measurement, derived from the classical theory on every occasion that empirical results do not satisfy our predictions. Lakatos[120] offers one way out, suggesting that certain laws and assertions may be treated as axiomatic within the framework of a research programme. Operationalism suggests that the measure defines what is being measured. The danger that lurks here is that we may lose sight of how adequately a measure captures the property that is of interest, since measurement must satisfy the tautology that it measures what it measures. On the other hand, it is difficult to see how we may have any meaningful notion of measurement quality if we are unable to define what is of interest (i.e. it is metaphysical).

immeasurable would seem to be an uneccessarily fraught enterprise — if not wilfully perverse.

It is singularly ironic that computer scientists should choose software complexity as their chief target for software metrics research. The consequence of claiming to measure the metaphysical has been a plethora of supposition, intuition, and instinct masquerading as general models of software and software construction. Without doubt, something is being measured, but what, and what it means, is quite unclear.

To summarize:

- Measurements must be made in the context of a model in order to have meaning and to admit validation.
- Models must address some problem or purpose.
- To be useful it is necessary to be able to relate the model to the 'real world', and this cannot be accomplished if it contains metaphysical entities. Consequently, operational definitions are required for all the endogenous and exogenous model variables.

Unfortunately, these points are very rarely addressed by metrics workers and, in particular, we note the predominance of implicitly informal and inadequately defined models, coupled with frequent reference to metaphysical variables such as complexity.

4.3.2 Models and theories

By now it should be clear that a model embodies a theory. This is expressed by the relationship between the inputs and the outputs of the model, and is the basis for useful models. It enables them to have predictive power. The most common form of theory within software metrics is that which is required to link direct measurement with phenomenon.

Referring back to our original illustration of temperature measurement, it will be recalled that mercury thermometers are affected by altitude and atmospheric pressure considerations. Additional measurements arc required in order to compensate for this complication. It is a general principle that as models are generalized across larger domains, so they require increasing numbers of inputs and they therefore grow in sophistication. Given our limited understanding of the software development process, it is an ambitious objective to continue to propose the type of all-encompassing, all-purpose, yet remarkably simplistic models that have abounded in the literature, for example Card and Agresti,[31] Halstead,[75] Henry,[82] and McCabe,[133] without consideration of the limitations and applicability of the model. By way of contrast, some cost estimation models, such as Boehm's COCOMO,[24] are relatively complex because they take into account explicitly the wide range of environments in which they may be used. For example, the detailed COCOMO model has more than 50 inputs and parameters.

This suggests an additional component to any useful model — that of its limitations. These are best expressed in terms of the assumptions that are made, thereby allowing the would-be user to determine its applicability to a particular problem domain. Where assumptions are deeply embedded, or merely implicit, this leads to difficulties in the validation and application of the model. Nowhere is this better illustrated than by some of the empirical work based on the Software Science model.[75] It is clear that this model assumes a small-scale programming* environment and a FORTRAN-like language. Arising from this assumption, is the fact that the meaning of 'effort' is self-evident — it is the time taken, usually no more than a few minutes, to develop the software.[†] Subsequent work, for instance by Basili and Phillips,[13] of large-scale, team-based software development highlights the ambiguities lurking behind the term 'effort'. For example, should requirements analysis be included, or, for that matter, changes in requirements during the development? Is time expended upon communication between team members to be included? How are library routines handled? What about fixing faults once the system has been released? It is thus not surprising that Basili reports a much weaker relationship between predicted and actual 'effort' than that found by earlier studies of very small-scale programs, for example Gordon and Halstead.[70]

The majority of criticisms of the Software Science model described in the precedingchapter are a direct consequence of violations of many of the implicit assumptions that Halstead made. Within the much smaller domain originally intended: of small algorithms, FORTRAN, and single programmer environments, the Software Science model might have had more chance of success, although other theoretical difficulties do remain.[40]

There is one outstanding ingredient for a model, and that is veracity. How much confidence can one have in the model and the measuring process that it supports? This may be expressed in a variety of ways, the most suitable being determined by the nature of the problem. One alternative is to specify the degree of accuracy, as in the COCOMO model where it is suggested that there is a 70% probability of the model being accurate to within plus or minus 20%.[24] Accuracy of design metrics also is given on occasions.[112, 179] Although confidence in our confidence is an intriguing philosophical (and recursive) problem it does not justify the widespread omission of this constituent of a model by software metrologists. Obviously, much empirical work is required to generate this data, but it is of great practical value, especially in a field such as software engineering where uncertainty is the order of the day.

---

*Indeed, Halstead was initially only concerned with algorithms.[74]

†Halstead and his colleagues were typically working with programs ranging from 7 to 59 lines of FORTRAN,[70] and averaging 24 LOC.

Despite the widespread reference to software modelling within the software metrics literature, there has been little discussion of the structure of a well-formed model. In this section we have argued that a model comprises: input and output variables; mappings between the 'real world' and the model thereby allowing 'real world' use; relationships linking inputs to outputs; assumptions that are made and, thus, delineation of the domains to be modelled; and some indication of the accuracy of model outputs. In addition, a model may contain parameters in order to enhance generalization capabilities. It is rare that all these components are even implicitly defined within a software model.

4.4 Model evaluation

Having scrutinized some of the deficiencies of existing software metrics and their underlying models, it is now appropriate to consider the desirable features of a metric. Although it is usual to speak of metric evaluation, strictly it is the model into which the metric enters that is validated. As has already been shown the model establishes the meaning of a metric. Without a model no evaluation is possible. It has also been demonstrated that a well-formed model has a number of components, for example parameters, some of which are frequently omitted or are, at the very least, deeply disguised. Evaluation of partial or poorly articulated models is unquestionably more difficult.

There should be two complementary approaches to model evaluation. First, the model may be analysed on a theoretical basis. In particular, one might search for the following characteristics:

- The model must conform to widely accepted theories of software development and cognitive science. Admittedly, this is a rather subjective criterion. However, consider the following example. A metric which predicts that a monolithic piece of software will have a lower incidence of errors than one divided into a number of modules must be viewed with suspicion. In such circumstances the onus would certainly be on the proponent to demonstrate the adequacy of the underlying theory.

- The model must be as formal as possible. In other words, the relationship between the input measurements and the output predictions must be precise in all situations. Furthermore, the mapping from the real world on to the model must be made as formal as possible.

- The model must use measurable inputs rather than estimates or subjective judgements. Failure to do so leads to inconsistencies between different users of the metric and potentially anomalous results.* Automation is not possible without satisfaction of this criterion.

---

*This seems to be a potential shortcoming of function points, *vide* Low and Jeffery.[129]

- The ordering of model evaluations is intentional, since meaningful empirical work is of questionable significance when based upon meaningless models of software. Therefore, theoretical analysis of the properties of a model ought to precede empirical validation. Furthermore, theoretical evaluation is often much quicker, and is consequently a cheaper and easier method of exposing some of the potential weaknesses in a model than is a full empirical study.

These rather general model attributes can be refined in order to provide a good deal more precision by means of the axiomatic approach.

A model should also be subjected to empirical evaluation. A model may have all the attributes listed above, satisfy a large set of axioms, and yet completely fail to describe the 'real world' that it purports to capture. Empirical validations are an equally necessary and complementary validation technique. In order that these may be meaningful they also require certain attributes. In brief the desiderata* are: large-scale empirical validations in a variety of different environments, particularly industrial environments; adequate controls so that it is possible for a null hypothesis to stand; and different teams of workers should be involved for statistical variability. These characteristics are described in more detail later in this chapter.

4.4.1 *Theoretical criteria*

To conclude this chapter it is worth examining some attempts which have been made to provide a framework whereby we can validate metrics theoretically. The two main strands of work are due to Weyuker and Prather; they both use an axiomatic technique.

In an attempt to provide some unifying framework for the evaluation of the extraordinarily divergent collection of software metrics, Prather[158] has proposed a set of axioms which a 'proper complexity metric' must satisfy. These are:

Axiom 4.1 *The complexity of the whole must not be less than the sum of the complexities of the parts.*

Axiom 4.2 *The complexity of a selection must be greater than the sum of all the branches, that is, the selection predicate must contribute to complexity.*

Axiom 4.3 *The complexity of an iteration must be greater than the iterated part.*

Although this is an interesting idea, a number of problems remain. First, the axioms are restricted to structured programs, since they do not address

---

*Of course, in an ideal world one would give full regard to all these factors. Unfortunately, in the world of limited resources that we happen to inhabit, compromises must often be made.

non-structured forms of control flow such as branching out of the middle of iterations. Second, the axioms are clearly aimed at a specific family of metrics, *viz* those that have underlying models based upon program control flow, for instance cyclomatic complexity[133] and the knot metric.[216] As a consequence they lack general applicability. Third, the axioms provide very little constraint upon the imaginations of the inventors of software metrics. It is true that Prather suggested upper bounds for Axioms 4.2 and 4.3 of twice the lower bound, but these seem to be more conjectures than axioms. No justification is offered to support these values.

Prather's approach can be characterized as a set of weak axioms for the family of control flow based metrics. Nowhere is this better demonstrated than by the impasse in which he finds himself when, having explicitly shown weaknesses in McCabe's metric, he is unable to evince any violation of his axiom set. Nevertheless, it represents an important new approach which has subsequently been developed further by others. It is important in that it provides a foundation for the comparison of essentially similar metrics. Also, it allows for the proscription of unacceptable model behaviours in a rather more formal fashion than has been current practice.

The first development of this work was by Fenton *et al.*[61] in order to extend the axiomatization to any procedural program, structured or otherwise. Program flow graphs are reduced to a hierarchy of irreducible graphs (prime trees) which permit any program structure to be defined uniquely. The axioms are redefined in terms of prime trees and thus made applicable to any procedural software. Subsequently, Prather[159] developed this work further, noting a distinction between hierarchically and recursively defined metrics, and marginally extending the scope of axioms defined over prime trees.[210]

Clearly, these are significant contributions to the problem of metric evaluation. The use of formalisms such as graph-theoretic approaches to modelling and metric definition facilitates reasoning about, and making comparisons between, models. Unfortunately the substance of the problem remains: the axiom sets are weak and the modelling incomplete. This is because the mappings from model to 'real world' are generally undefined or ill-defined. The latter is the price paid for formality: that the more formal you get the more difficult it is to fit reality.* There is also an additional problem concerning closure of the concatenation operation to which we will be return in due course.

A contrasting perspective is due to Weyuker,[209] who presents a set of nine axioms or properties that a well-formed 'complexity measure' and its underlying model should satisfy. These axioms might be regarded as strong, in the sense that they impose considerable restrictions upon the

---

*'As far as the laws of mathematics refer to reality, they are not certain; and as far as they are certain, they do not refer to reality.' *A. Einstein.*

scope of permissible metrics. This is borne out by the observation that none of the metrics evaluated by Weyuker satisfy more than seven out of nine axioms. For programs p, q and r,* where | | denotes a hypothetical measuring function yielding a non-negative number and pr the set of all programs, the axioms are:

Axiom 4.4 *The measure must not assign the same number to all programs:*

$$\exists p, q \in pr \bullet |p| \neq |q| \qquad (4.4)$$

Axiom 4.5 *There exist only a countable number of programs for a given measurement value.*

To judge this one, needs to make certain assumptions concerning the programming language and the target machine. The stated purpose of this axiom is to 'strengthen' the first axiom, as violation suggests that the measure is comparatively insensitive.

Axiom 4.6 *There are programs drawn from the same equivalence class:*

$$\exists p, q \in pr \bullet |p| = |q| \qquad (4.5)$$

Axiom 4.7 *There must exist programs that compute the same function but have different numbers attached to them.*

As Weyuker notes, for all practical purposes the first and fourth axioms are equivalent.

Axiom 4.8 *The measure must be monotonic:*

$$\forall p, q \in pr \bullet |p| \leq |p \circ q| \wedge |q| \leq |p \circ q| \qquad (4.6)$$

This axiom centres around the meaning ascribed to the concatenation operation $\circ$ for the object or process being measured. For many software metrics it is not self-evident how to define this operation, a point that we will return to later.

Axiom 4.9 *Concatenation of a program r to another program must not always yield a constant increment to the total program measure:*

$$\exists p, q, r \in pr \bullet |p| = |q| \wedge |r \circ p| \neq |r \circ q| \qquad (4.7)$$

Also:

$$\exists p, q, r \in pr \bullet |p| = |q| \wedge |p \circ r| \neq |q \circ r| \qquad (4.8)$$

This not a universal desideratum of software measurement. For example, consider the measurement of LOC, the issue depends upon the choice of measurement scale type, as described earlier in this chapter.

Axiom 4.10 *The measure must be sensitive to the ordering of the program components.*

---

*While Weyuker talks in terms of programs, clearly, one could substitute any measurement object.

If q is some permutation of p, then:

$$\exists p, q \in pr \bullet |p| \neq |q| \tag{4.9}$$

Our comments concerning the preceding axiom are also applicable here.

Axiom 4.11 *The measure must be insensitive to renaming changes of program components.*

Thus, if p is a renaming of q, then

$$\forall p, q \in pr \bullet |p| = |q| \tag{4.10}$$

As Weyuker herself observes, this is only appropriate for syntactic measures. If we were concerned with cognitive complexity or programming style, naming might be thought to be highly significant.

Axiom 4.12 *The measure must permit synergistic concatenations:*

$$\forall p, q \in pr \bullet |p| + |q| < |p \circ q| \tag{4.11}$$

This is a generalized form of Prather's second and third axioms since the type of component remains unspecified, but also more stringent as the axiom demands, rather than accepts, synergy.

Weyuker's axiom set is considerably more restrictive than Prather's but this, in turn, creates complications. The properties that are required of a measure depend, to a large degree, upon its purpose and the type of scale adopted. In developing a general axiom set, one is confronted by a dilemma. The axiom set is either generalized but weak, as in the Prather approach, or more restrictive but rejects measures on grounds that are believed to be desirable, as in the case of Weyuker's axioms. The latter point can be demonstrated with regard to her second axiom. Suppose there is a design metric which assigns a value to a particular design. From this design we are able to generate an infinite number of possible programs that implement it, and thus the metric violates the axiom since it demands that there be at most a finite number of programs for a given measurement value. No design measure is therefore able to fully satisfy her axiom set; manifestly an unacceptable position to adopt.

Consider, also, her fifth axiom concerning the property of monotonicity. Whether this is desirable depends upon the measurement scale adopted; for nominal scales it would be inappropriate. It is also dependent upon the meaning of concatenation, as has already been remarked, and in particular whether we admit closure or not.[118, 131] This is important for data flow metrics[150] and information flow metrics,[31, 82, 177] where, by adding extra program components, one might decrease the measure because the measures are based on inter-modular or block flows. Weyuker presents such an example.[209] The problem is: do we allow the concatenation of any group of program components to any other group of components? The answer must be no for two reasons. First, measures of syntactically incorrect programs are meaningless. Second, for non-code metrics, such as design, the components of interest are not program statements. Consequently, there is no closure of concatenation and, therefore, the fifth axiom is not universally applicable to software measures.

4.4.2 *Empirical criteria*

A recurring theme in the history of software metrics — and of the preceding chapter — has been the presentation of empirical 'evidence' supporting a metric, only for a rebuttal to be published a few years later. This is well exemplified by Hamer and Frewin's critique[77] of much of the empirical work claiming to support the Software Science model. The question therefore arises: are there any general criteria by which empirical validations may be judged?

In a review of empirical validations of design metrics, Ince and Shepperd[89] isolate three general factors which are pertinent for the assessment of empirical validations. They are:

- the hypothesis under investigation;

- the artificiality of the data used;

- the validity of the statistics employed.

These criteria will now be examined in more detail. Probably the most serious and commonplace charge that can be levelled at empirical work is that it is seldom clear what is being validated. This arises from imprecise, incomplete, or more commonly, metaphysical models. In such situations effort would be better directed at the model, and the development of an unambiguous hypothesis, rather than launching into an empirical validation. The efficacy of this is confirmed by the empirical study by Ince and Shepperd[90] of the information flow metric.[82] Here, initial work removing anomalies and inconsistencies from the underlying model was rewarded by greatly improved empirical results, and statistically meaningful results obtained from the 'cleaned up' model. It must be stressed again that statistically meaningful empirical results derived from a meaningless model are in themselves meaningless.

The second criterion of an empirical validation has, in turn, three dimensions. These are the number of data points (ideally a large number), the type of environment (ideally an industrial environment producing large-scale software systems), and the type of staff (ideally professional software engineers as opposed to students). Applying this criterion to generate a five-point classification of design metric validations, Ince and Shepperd[89] found less than 10% to be fully satisfactory, and more than 50% of studies investigated received the lowest classification of the scale. Subsequently, the situation has improved slightly, but it still leaves much to be desired.

Statistical validity is the third criterion by which to evaluate an empirical validation. First, and foremost, is the need for any evaluation to be capable of refuting the hypothesis under investigation. Randomly searching for statistically significant correlations is almost certain to unearth some relationship. However, in the absence of a clearly defined hypothesis derived from the model under study, claims of causality must be viewed as extremely tenuous. Careful controls and 'null' hypotheses are methods for making it possible to refute a hypothesis. Use of LOC as a benchmark for comparison with other metrics[12] is another possibility. It also introduces the possibility of statistical alternatives to correlation coefficients, for instance tests to see if data points are drawn from the same population.*

Tests of correlation are also vulnerable to problems of dependence between the dependent variable and external variables, as in the case of McCabe's cyclomatic complexity measure[176] and Yin and Winchester's graph impurity measure.[89, 219] In both instances the measures correlate more strongly with program length than with the program attributes they purport to measure. Program length, in turn, correlates with program attributes. What is almost certainly occurring is that cyclomatic complexity, graph impurity, and the program attributes are all dependent on program length. There is a causal association from length to attribute but not, or only very weakly, from cyclomatic complexity or graph impurity to attribute. The celebrated example is, of course, the correlation between the spatial distribution of prostitutes and ministers of religion where there is no causality (or at least one hopes not!), but, rather, the independent influence of demographic factors (i.e. they both cluster around urban areas).

Inappropriateness of statistical technique is another source of difficulty. This reveals itself most frequently as the use of statistics that assume normal data distributions when such assumptions cannot be justified. The empirical validation by Henry and Kafura[82, 103] applied the parametric Pearson correlation test to the information flow metric that contains a quadratic term and is consequently highly skewed. A non-parametric test would have been more suitable. Yin and Winchester fall foul of a similar problem. Removal of four outlier data points reduces their correlation coefficient from 0.98 to 0.52.[219, 178] Statistics that are meaningless for the type of measurement scale can also lead to confusion.

Selectivity of data points can be another problem area for empirical validations. Henry and Kafura eliminate four data points from their study, where their model fails to predict adequately, on the basis that the modules were too complex to be changed.[84] However, this appears to be a deficiency of their model and is therefore unwarranted. A more common practice is the elimination of zero scoring data points, typically modules that do not

---

*Examples are the Student t test for parametric data and the Mann-Whitney U test for non-parametric data.

contain errors. Again, this is a statistically dubious practice as there is no way in which these data points may be identified *a priori*.

This review of empirical practices may have painted a rather pessimistic picture. The criteria outlined describe an ideal empirical evaluation. In reality there exist constraints of cost, time, and availability of data. It is therefore appropriate to distinguish between those features that one might regard as mandatory and those which are merely desirable. Any empirical validation must address an unambiguous hypothesis, be capable of refuting it, and use statistically sound techniques. Representative data points are clearly advantageous, but this criterion must sometimes, of necessity, be relaxed. In doing so the onus remains upon the researchers to demonstrate that any results obtained translate to other, less artificial, environments.

This section on model evaluation has described what must be construed as almost a wish list. It is concluded that evaluating software models is altogether more difficult than might be supposed. Consequently, it is more appropriate to address smaller and more manageable problems. The search for 'Holy Grail'-type metrics would not seem to be either productive or feasible at the present time.

4.5   Summary

This section has had two aims. First, it has examined the role of modelling and measurement and looked at the difficult subject of the evaluation of software metrics. Second it has examined two approaches used for theoretical evaluation due to Weyuker and Prather. The concept of axiomatization of measurement is powerful. It allows a formal description of desired and undesired model behaviours, which is invaluable for the theoretical evaluation of metrics and their associated models. Unfortunately, neither the weak nor the strong axiom sets that have been presented in this chapter are sufficient for even a significant subset of software metrics. It is therefore necessary to consider the new approach of tailored axiomatization. This is the purpose of the next chapter.

5

AN APPROACH TO METRICS MODELLING

Synopsis

So far in this monograph we have described a number of serious problems that afflict the metrics area. Also, in the preceding chapter, we have examined some ways in which researchers have attempted to put the study of metrics on a more formal footing. This chapter first examines a promising recent approach to metrics development — the GQM method — and then outlines our approach to metrics development. This approach is based on adapting the axiomatic approach outlined in the preceding chapter and modifying the GQM method. We present a small, artificial example to describe the approach.

5.1 The development of software metrics

There has been little effort directed towards development methods for software metrics, in part due to the belated realization of the problems involved in the field. Two of the few contributions of significance are the Goal – Question – Metric (GQM) paradigm of Victor Basili *et al.*[15, 16, 165] and the constructive quality model (COQUAMO) methodology,[110] which employs a similar hierarchic approach based around software quality factors, criteria and metrics. However, given the importance of the model for software measurement, GQM is only a partial methodology. In the final parts of this chapter we extend this metric development methodology so that it recognizes the central role of a model explicitly; and this is illustrated by a simple example. A fuller example is presented Chapter 6.

5.1.1 *The Goal/Question/Metric paradigm*

The GQM paradigm for software metrics[16, 166] is based on the fact that measurement is carried out for a purpose, and that only within the context of a purpose or goal can it be determined which metrics might be useful. The approach can be characterized as top–down, and is in marked contrast to the current practice of obtaining a metric and then hunting around for some meaning.

The primary question to ask is 'What is the measurement goal?'. A goal has the following attributes:

- an object of interest which may be either a product or a process;

- a purpose such as understanding, characterizing or improving;

- a perspective that identifies who is interested in the results, for example management, software developers or the customer;

- a description of the environment to give a proper context to any results.

The next step is to refine a goal (or goals) into one or more questions. This is a process of substituting metaphysical concepts such as 'complexity' and 'quality' by more concrete and measurable, i.e. phenomenological, definitions. The danger inherent in a top-down approach is that goals may be set that cannot be easily satisfied, and some concepts may defy translation into more specific and quantifiable questions.[166] In these circumstances *omissions should be noted as they have considerable bearing upon the subsequent interpretation of results*. It may also be appropriate to review the original goals. Having identified a set of questions, metrics are derived to determine what must be measured in order to answer each question.

The outcome is a hierarchy of goals, questions, and metrics, where there is a many-to-many mapping from goal to question, and from question to metric. The strength of this paradigm is that every metric is placed in the a context of answering a question in order to meet a measurement goal. Furthermore, metrics are only identified to satisfy particular goals or objectives. Rombach[165, 166] describes the successful application of GQM to an investigation of maintenance problems experienced by the Burroughs Corporation.

The establishment of measurement goals by the GQM paradigm is the first step of the Basili *et al.* methodology. The next stage is to plan the measurement process by stating explicitly any hypotheses and to design data collection techniques, building in validation checks as far as is possible. The third step is collecting the measurements, with the final step in the cycle, according to Basili, being interpretation.

Despite the seeming simplicity of the GQM paradigm, it must be viewed as a major advance for software metrics. In particular, it forces problem definition followed by the identification of those metrics necessary to provide answers. Further, GQM provides a context both to understand the meaning and to evaluate metrics — something that is all too often lacking in work in this field. It is also an extremely flexible approach, and one which may easily be applied to almost any aspect of software engineering measurement.

Modelling, or rather the lack of, is the only reservation that one has concerning the methodology. Although the identification of hypotheses suggests that there must be some underlying model, this is insufficient considering the central role of the model within metrology. As a consequence, we have modified the GQM approach so as to provide for explicit modelling and evaluation.*

5.2   Tailored axioms

Before looking at our metrics development method it is worth describing
its basis: that of tailored axioms. In order to steer a course between the
Scylla of weak, undiscriminative axiom sets, and the Charybdis of strong,
restrictive axiom sets for acceptable software metrics and their underlying
models, it is necessary to tailor axioms to specific measures and models.[†]
   Measures must satisfy three classes of axioms:

- those axioms that are fundamental to all measurement;
- axioms necessary for the type of scale adopted;
- axioms specific to the model underlying the measure.

It is also vitally important that measures are fit for the purpose for which
they are intended. It will be noted that the axiom classes decrease in scope
of application from universal to specific for a single, or small family of
metrics. Each class will be reviewed in turn.

   The following are axioms that must hold for all measurement if it is to
be meaningful.

Axiom 5.1 *It must be possible to describe, even if not formally, the rules
governing the measurement.*[154] *Once the error-proneness of the measuring
process has been accounted for, all measurements of the same object or
process must assign it to the same equivalence class.*[‡]

This axiom is somewhat difficult to apply in practice.

Axiom 5.2 *The measure must generate at least two equivalence classes.*

This is in order that, as Weyuker[209] points out, the measure be capable of
discrimination.

Axiom 5.3 *An equality relation is required.*

This is similar in impact to Weyuker's third axiom.[209] Without an empirical
equality operation, each measurement, if it could be called that, would
generate a new equivalence class with exactly one member.

---

*Although we concentrate on GQM in this chapter and cite it as one of the most
mature metrics development methods there is evidence that some metrics researchers
are beginning to concentrate on modelling.[170]

[†]An alternative, flexible approach has been presented by Zuse and Bollmann[223, 222]
in the form of viewpoints which allow for the specification of varying sets of fundamental
requirements for different metrics, or even the same metric. The method described in
this book differs in that it employs an equational rewrite system to define and reason
with the axioms.

[‡]This does not imply that the rules must always be applied correctly, since there
is the possibility of error in the measurement process — a point eloquently made by
Kyberg,[119] among others.

Axiom 5.4 *If an infinite number of objects or events is measured, eventually two or more must be assigned to the same equivalence class, that is, you can't measure an infinite number of objects.*

This is a restatement of Weyuker's third axiom.[209] We note that some forms of measurement that uses a nominal scale, for example car number plates, do not satisfy this axiom — hardly a surprising observation when one considers that such a process must lie at the limits of what could reasonably be called measurement.

Axiom 5.5 *The metric must not produce anomalies, that is, the metric must preserve empirical orderings.*

In other words the Representation Theorem[118, 199] must hold:

$$\forall p, q \in object \bullet Pr_e Q \Rightarrow |P|r_n|Q| \qquad (5.1)$$

where r_e is any empirically observable relation and r_n is the equivalent relation within the number or measurement system.

Axiom 5.6 *The Uniqueness Theorem must hold[199] for all permissible transformations for the particular scale type, that is, there is a homomorphism between the transformed and the measurement structures.*

The second class of axioms, those that are sufficient for different measurement scales, are well documented in the classical measurement literature, for example Stevens[193] and Krantz *et al.*,[118] and have already been reviewed earlier in this chapter. Clearly, our axiom set must be tailored to take account of scale, and this is a fundamental decision for the software metrologist.

The third class of axioms are those that relate to the specific model underlying the measure in question. Again, it is possible to provide categories under which axioms may be selected. These are:

- resolution;
- empirically meaningful structures;
- model invariants.

Under resolution it may be desirable to include Weyuker's second axiom, which asserts that there only exists a finite number of objects of a given measurement score. This would be important if metrics insensitive, in certain respects,* are to be avoided. Having chosen the axioms necessary for the type of measurement, one must consider the concatenation operations available for the objects or processes under scrutiny. The importance of concatenation is that it is the constructor operator and it allows us to

---

*The classic example, is of course, McCabe's cyclomatic complexity,[133] where one may vary infinitely the number of procedure nodes for a fixed number of predicate nodes, for a program flow graph.

describe different objects or processes in a recursive[61] or hierarchical[159] manner. What the existing approaches fail to embrace is the possibility of metrics where there is no concatenation closure.* This is an important aspect of any axiomatization: that we define meaningless structures where any measurement operation remains undefined or is described using three-valued logic in a manner similar to that outlined by Suppes.[198]

Model invariants are clearly going to be extremely diverse. Examples include Prather's second and third axioms, which relate to measures of control flow structure.[158] This is a difficult aspect of an axiomatic evaluation of a model because, in the end, the choice of axioms will be dependent upon intuition and insight. Where it cannot be shown that a model satisfies such an axiom, two conclusions are possible.

First, one might infer that the model is deficient in some respect, or, second, that the axiom itself is inappropriate. Whatever is true, this axiomatic method at least draws the attention of the metrologist to such potential problem areas. It does not necessarily provide an answer.

In concluding this section it is worth making three points. First, axiomatizations of software metrics are a vital tool for the theoretical validation of metrics and models, as they allow exploration of the model behaviour in a more rigorous fashion. Without doubt, they represent a step forward from merely using one's intuition. They may also permit a more thorough coverage of the model behaviour than the intuitive approach or, for that matter, than many empirical evaluations, particularly where cost or availability of data is a factor.

Second, they provide a mechanism with which to establish certain foundational properties of the model. These are:

- consistency — so that there exists one and only one outcome for any set of inputs;
- completeness — that the axiom set is sufficiently rich that there is no set of inputs for which no outcome is prescribed;
- the model is not rejected for violation of axioms for empirically meaningless structures.

Consistency is established by showing that the axiom set exhibits the Church–Rosser property. This is, unfortunately, an undecidable question. There are various notions of completeness, including the Liskov–Guttag concept of sufficiently complete[125] which is weaker than the more usual mathematical definitions of completeness† but these are still undecidable.

Third, theoretical evaluation provides early feedback for the design and development of metrics and models. Given that empirical validation is a

---

*This will be the case for any syntactic software metric.

†An axiom set is usually said to be complete if it is impossible to add an independent axiom because all well-formed formulae either follow from, or are inconsistent with, the existing axiom set.

costly and time-consuming enterprise, any technique that helps to identify models that are manifestly inadequate must be lauded.

5.2.1 *A model-based methodology for metric development*

Since a model is at the heart of the comprehension of a problem, and provides the means whereby we exclude such irrelevant and unimportant factors as noise in order to concentrate upon those factors that are believed to be significant,* the construction of a model ought to be at the core of a metrics methodology. Moreover, the methodology must incorporate model evaluation and iteration where required. Software engineering processes and products are comparatively poorly understood so review and refinement must be anticipated.

Figure 5.1 presents the various stages of the methodology. This diagram suggests that there is a one-to-one mapping between a problem and a model. Obviously, this need not be the case. Some problems may be best addressed by several models, and one model may be useful for a multiplicity of problems. The latter is suggestive of the need for the reuse of models or parts of models. In the past this has been hindered by poorly and incompletely articulated models. As more structure is introduced into the modelling process, so the prospect of model and measurement re-use becomes more of a realistic possibility. The stages of metric development identified by the method will be discussed in turn. These are also presented in Shepperd.[180]

In the same way as the GQM paradigm,[16] our method recognizes that the first and fundamental stage is to examine purpose. The problems associated with modelling in a vacuum have already been rehearsed. Without a sense of purpose there are no means of determining what should, and should not, be incorporated within a model. Any description of the problem should include information concerning the problem domain. There is a considerable difference between predicting error-prone modules at the design stage for a one-person software house producing only simple computer games, and for the much wider domain of all software engineering activity. Problems in the latter category are unlikely to be solved easily. The problem description also needs to make clear whose problem is being solved. A company director may have a different view of productivity from the software engineer.

The next stage is to construct an informal model of the application area to be measured. Intuitions and existing software engineering knowledge is brought to bear upon the problem in order to identify those factors that are perceived as being important. At this stage many of the factors will be

---

*We may also recognize that they are meaningful but temporarily ignore them to make progress. We feel that the biggest error in current metrics work is to gather together and analyse too much data in one large step. Advances in metrics work — if they are to be solidly based — must be step-by-step

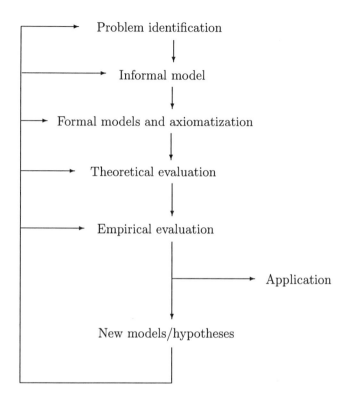

FIG. 5.1. The stages of the metrics methodology.

metaphysical because they lack operational definitions (e.g. maintainability, ease of comprehension, etc.).

A crucial part of transforming an informal into a formal model is fixing it
into the 'real world' by defining the mappings between the model variables
and the reality that they purport to capture. The definitions must be
consistent with the original problem definition, otherwise there is a danger
of diluting the problem into something else, merely because it is easier to
define or understand. At the hub of a model are the relationships that
it expresses between the input and output variables. In defining these it
is often appropriate to axiomatize the model so as to describe the desired
model behaviour unambiguously.

An axiom set will also simplify the subsequent theoretical evaluation
of the model. Depending upon the problem domain, it may be desirable
to introduce parameters into the model so as to increase its scope. The
remaining two components of a well-formed model are a list of assumptions
that will characterize our understanding of the problem domain, and the

desired level of accuracy. The latter may be obtained from the problem description. Comparison with actual levels of accuracy will help in the empirical evaluation of a model, and will provide a valuable basis for the comparison of competing models.

The stages of theoretical and empirical model evaluation have already been described fully in the early parts of this and the preceding chapter. However, it should be stressed that model building is an iterative exercise, and provision ought to be made for backtracking. In particular, our method emphasizes theoretical evaluation, as it is usually much quicker and less costly than empirical analysis of a model. It is entirely reasonable to suggest that the cheaper 'testing' be performed first. It is not suggested that theoretical evaluation should be a substitute for empirical work, as both are likely to uncover different types of problems.* For example, theoretical analysis using axioms might detect 'pathological' structures for which the model produces inappropriate behaviours. On the other hand, an empirical analysis might detect significant factors that are not included within the model.

The penultimate stage identified is application. This suggests that the model has satisfied certain theoretical and empirical criteria and, therefore, depending upon the type of problem, is deemed suitable for wider and less critical use. Evaluation of the model ought not to cease once this stage is achieved, but it is regarded in a different light to the evaluation stages, in order to draw attention to the distinction between nascent, and therefore rather tentative, models, and those that have acquired rather more maturity and, therefore, reliability. It is not easy to think of many models that could currently be placed in the latter category — except possibly some of the function point approaches that have been tuned for particular organizational environments.[2, 200] The final stage is to refine the model based either on factors that have been ignored or on the empirical evaluation.

As with the vast majority of software engineering methods, this approach is not prescriptive. Its contribution is to focus attention upon important issues, in this case modelling, and identify a set of smaller steps that lead towards the construction of an adequately evaluated model.

5.2.2 *An example*

It must be stressed at the outset of this example that it is intended purely to illustrate the metric development methodology, and not to provide deep insights into the problems of software maintenance. Consequently, the example is a gross simplification and is not offered as a useful model. The following two chapters provide more realistic examples of a software design

---

*One of the best papers which support the need for good empirical validation has been produced by Kitchenham.[113]

model.

The starting point for the development of a software metric is the identification of a problem. Let us assume that we are interested in maintenance, and wish to be able to identify hard-to-maintain systems whilst still at the design stage of developing software. This ability is only required in the restricted domain of a small software house, producing very homogeneous, interactive, information-retrieval systems. The required level of accuracy for prediction is the identification of 75% of the systems that fall into the upper quartile of systems ranked by maintainability. Although even at this early stage we note that software maintainability has no operational definition, we postpone addressing this issue — other than by observing that our perspective will be that of the software engineer — until after we have begun to construct a prototype or informal model.

Now to develop the informal model. What factors do we think have a significant bearing upon maintainability within the problem domain? Remembering that this is a simplified example, it might be conjectured that there is a relationship between the number of database references that a system makes, normalized for system size, and the ease of its maintenance. In other words, we are concerned with the density of references. The informal model has identified two input variables, a database reference count and system size, that are related to the output variable maintainability. We have:

$$M = f(r/s) \tag{5.2}$$

where M is maintainability, r is the count of database references and s is system size. As is frequently the case, $f(r/s)$ is an indirect measure of M, since temporal considerations preclude it from being measured directly.

The next stage is the development of a formal model and an axiomatization of desired behaviour. At the risk of being repetitive, it must be emphasized that software maintainability currently has no operational definition. We are not, therefore, in a position to measure maintainability, and it is arguable, then, that it is a metaphysical attribute and must, as a result, be refined into terms that are directly observable. If we are unable to do so, the model cannot be anchored in reality. For simplicity's sake we will reduce our concept of maintainability to that of the percentage of modules modified per unit time per defect removed, where the most obvious unit of time is a software release.

The implication of this is that a low percentage suggests that the maintenance changes have been accommodated easily (high maintainability), while a high percentage suggests a software structure that is highly resistant to modification (low maintainability). Three areas require further refinement. First, what constitutes a system release; second what is a change to a module; and third when are the measurements made? A possible definition is any alteration that requires any part of the text of the entire software system source code to be altered in any way leading to the generation of a new version. A module change can be viewed as any change to the text within the module bounds. As regards timing of measurements, the measure of version n of the system is intended to be an indirect measure of the cost of transforming the system into version $n + 1$. The consequence of this transformation, or maintenance action, is to potentially modify the future maintainability so that the transformation from version $n + 1$ to $n + 2$ may be more or less difficult, since the database reference density may have been modified. Whether our measure is acceptable as an indicator of maintainability is open to question. However, at least we are making plain what is, and is not, being measured by the model.

The mapping from 'real world' on-to the model, in the form of database reference counts r and system size s must also be defined. A database is defined as any system modifiable data (i.e. not constants, type definitions etc.) that is shared by two or more modules. A reference is either the retrieval from, or the updating of, a database. It might be appropriate at this stage to enquire as to whether such information is available at the design stage. If it is not, our emerging model will not be able to solve the problem that it is being developed for. System size s will be the count of modules comprising the system. We note, parenthetically, the implicit assumption that modules are relatively homogeneous, otherwise module count may be a poor choice for system size.

Finally, we require some definitions. The code realization of a module will have the following properties:

- components grouped lexically and visible to the software engineer either within the program text or in a library which he or she is able to update (this excludes compiler defined modules such as the Pascal readln);

- identifiable bounds, for example begin ... end;

- be referenced by name, from other parts of the program/system;

- return execution to the calling software after elaboration.

The precise details of a module are obviously language dependent as, for example, a COBOL module paragraph or section will be very different from an Ada package. From this definition, it is evident that the model in its present form is not applicable to non-procedural languages such as PROLOG. Again, it is assumed that a design or system architecture will identify all the modules, and that there is at least a close approximation between the designed architecture and the realized architecture.

A database reference is defined as either a read or write access to a data object that is not private to a single module; in other words it is accessed by at least two separate modules. Furthermore, at least one access must be a write access. This, therefore, excludes constants.

Although some of the above definitions may be contentious, or capable of refinement, they are at least made explicit. It is apparent that even a simple concept such as a module requires careful thought and definition in practice. For this reason software metrologists might be better advised to concentrate upon simpler and more manageable metrics than software complexity metrics.

The model may now be expressed more formally as:

$$m_c/m = f(r/m) \qquad (5.3)$$

where m_c is the number of modules changed per system release and m is the total number of modules. The next step is to try to define f, which is a calibration function linking the indirect measures to the m_c/m. Before we do this it is helpful to delineate acceptable model behaviours by means of axioms. A three-layered approach to flexible axiomatization has already been outlined in this chapter, where the first set of axioms comprise those that are common to all measurement, the second those that are necessary for the chosen measurement scale (as yet undecided because f is undefined), and, the third those that are specific to the model. It is the last category that we wish to address.

Understanding the model behaviour focuses upon the empirical meaning we attach to the concatenation of systems. Indeed, what is the fundamental constructor operation? The primitive or indivisible components of a system that concern us are modules and database references. These can be described formally using grammar rules which define all syntactically valid concatenations. Module calling is also introduced into the grammar, because it is part of a complete system architecture, even if it does not enter explicitly into our model of software maintenance.

The grammar for our abstract system architecture notation, using an extended form of BNF,[*] is as follows:

system::= (module) (databasename)
module::=modname [(modcall)] [(databaseref)]

Technically, the grammar is ambiguous, but since we have no intention of parsing it, this is of little concern. A concatenation is now defined as:

$$concat : system \times token \rightarrow system \cup \{error\} \qquad (5.4)$$

where a token can be any terminal from the above grammar. An error condition or undefined state results from any syntactically incorrect concatenation operation. The advantage of this approach as compared to that

---

[*]Terminals are in sans-serif typeface and non-terminals are in italic serif. Parentheses indicate zero or more iterations and square brackets indicate optional elements.

of Prather[158, 159] or Fenton *et al.*,[61] is that the non-closure of concatenation is catered for explicitly. However, there remains the problem of a context-dependent grammar, for example a database reference to an undefined database. This is unimportant for our model, but there does exist a number of formalisms suitable for the specification of the semantics of a grammar, such as the algebraic or axiomatic methods.[72, 125] These represent the behaviour of the model, or what mathematicians would call a theory, as an algebra where the axioms of such a system are rewrite rules. The following chapter employs these methods for the model of system architecture.

Having established the groundwork, the desired model behaviour can now be dealt with in more detail where p and q are systems.

Axiom 5.7 *The addition of database references must always increase the measurement value of m_c:*

$$\forall p \in sys; d \in dbr \bullet |p \circ d| > |p| \qquad (5.5)$$

where sys is the set of all possible systems and dbr is the set of all database references. This implies that multiple references by a module to the same database will be counted more than once.

Axiom 5.8 *The addition of non-database reference components (modules or database declarations) will have no impact upon m_c:*

$$\forall p \in sys; m \in mn \bullet |p \circ m| = |p| \qquad (5.6)$$

where mn is the set of all module names, or

$$\forall p \in sys; d \in dnm \bullet |p \circ d| = |p| \qquad (5.7)$$

where dnm is the set of all database names. This has the interesting implication that a system may be infinitely large but make no database references and, therefore, minimize maintenance problems. As this is a simplified model this need not concern us except in one respect, that of the minimum maintenance change.

Axiom 5.9 *Since a system release has been defined as a change, this must be contained in at least one module:*

$$\forall p \in sys \bullet |p| \geq 1 \qquad (5.8)$$

Axiom 5.10 *The worst case for the maintenance measure is when all modules are modified:*

$$\forall p \in sys \bullet |p| \leq m \qquad (5.9)$$

Even without formal proofs of consistency of the axiom set the conflict between the third and fourth axioms can be seen. There exist situations, for instance architectures containing a single module, where the addition of database references will not increase the metric. Thus, the first axiom must be relaxed somewhat or the model must be reformulated. A more minor point is that the metric must yield integers because there is no empirical counterpart to a partial module! The strength of this, rather theoretical, approach is that problems of model behaviour are identified early on, and explicit decisions are made. The fundamental point is not what is the best decision, but the fact that the decision must be incorporated within the model. It is unsatisfactory to omit this information which leads to different individuals making different interpretations.

A final axiom is required before f can be fully identified.

Axiom 5.11 *The addition of a database reference will always have the same impact upon the metric, irrespective of the number of references made, subject only to the limitations to m_c described above.*

$$\forall p, q \in sys; d : dbr \bullet (|p \circ d| - |p|) = (|q \circ d| - |q|) \qquad (5.10)$$

subject to $1 \leq m_c \leq m$.

From this we may deduce that function f will be linear* within the range $1 \ldots m$ and so will have the general form:

$$\alpha + \beta(r)$$

The axioms give little clue to the values for the coefficients α and β, other than that β must be greater than zero. In practice, there exists a greater interplay between the different stages of the methodology than might first be apparent. Almost inevitably, recourse to empirical analysis is required in order to provide specific values for the coefficients. Were the model to be extended to different domains it is likely that different values would be required.

At this stage we can consider the type of scale and unit with which we are dealing. Clearly, $\alpha + \beta(r)$ leads to an interval scale. This can be demonstrated by the fact that the following empirical operations are available:

- determination of equality;
- determination of greater or less;
- determination of equality of intervals;

but not determination of equality of ratios.

The transformations that do not result in the loss of ordering are similarity and linear transformations. Such observations may appear trivial in this instance; however, this is not necessarily so for some of the other metrics that have been proposed and, indeed, the absence of any obvious

---

*The axiom of linearity has profound implications upon the model and causes potential complications concerning the satisfaction of $1 \leq m_c \leq m$. A curvilinear relationship would seem both more plausible and convenient.

empirical additive operation makes the determination of scale and unit an area of difficulty.

The assumptions that the model makes are that modules are of roughly equal size. It is also assumed that database references are generally homogeneous, and that all module maintenance changes are comparable. Furthermore, we must assume that implemented systems do reflect their designs and we have not considered the possibility that maintenance changes may involve the addition of new modules or the removal of existing modules.

Having established the necessary theoretical foundations it is now appropriate to investigate our model of software maintenance empirically. For this to take place suitable hypotheses need to be established and the necessary data collection carried out. We must also establish how error-prone this measurement process is, and its limitations. Empirical work will also enable us to see the sort of restrictions that our assumptions place upon the model — the worst case being that they render the model unworkable. As has been suggested, model building is an iterative process, so, as our understanding matures, additional factors are incorporated into the model and the estimates for the coefficients are refined. In this way we are slowly able to proceed to the perception of software engineering as an activity that consumes multiple resources and engineers, and software systems as entities that have multiple facets to be characterized.[102] This, then, necessitates the collection of more than two metrics in order to measure maintainability indirectly.

Even the simplified example of a maintainability model presented here has demonstrated that software modelling is not a trivial process and that it has many ramifications. This, in itself, is a compelling reason for the adoption of a little more rigour, and for an attempt to eliminate at least some undesirable model properties early on in the development of software metrics. The attendant reduction in heartache and wasted effort by those attempting to validate metrics might be regarded as a bonus.

5.3 Summary

This chapter has formed an introduction to the remainder of this book. It has briefly described the GQM method for developing software metrics. It has shown that this method lacks a modelling dimension, and described how this could be incorporated by means of an axiomatic approach. However, an important feature is that the axiomatic approach outlined here is tailored towards the particular metric that is being derived.

6

A UNI-DIMENSIONAL MODEL OF DESIGN

Synopsis

In the absence of a clearly articulated model, software measurement is a fruitless exercise. In the preceding chapter we sought to remedy this situation by proposing a method to aid the development and evaluation of software metrics, together with their underlying models. This was illustrated by an extremely simple example. This chapter describes a larger software engineering problem for which we develop a model to relate software design to the quality factors of implementability, reliability, and maintainability. A formal model is developed and evaluated using the apparatus of the method outlined in the preceding chapter. Each step in the development of the model is outlined: problem identification, construction of an informal model, statement of the formal model, and axiomatization of the model. This is followed by theoretical and empirical validations. The chapter concludes that more than one model input — or multi-dimensional modelling — is necessary to improve the model performance and provide useful support for the software engineer carrying out design tasks. It is important to point out that in this chapter we are not attempting to promote one system design metric, but, rather, are using a particular metric as an example of the metric development process that was described in the preceding chapter.

6.1 Restatement of the problem

In this section the first two stages of the development of a model are given consideration. Fundamental to this is the identification of the problem, if only because modelling the universe, or even just that subset related to software engineering, is an ambitious undertaking! The problem statement is then refined into an informal model. As the chapter title makes clear, our model is characterized as a uni-dimensional model based upon a single input. This somewhat simplistic approach is adopted intentionally for two reasons. First, the empirical validation of multi-dimensional models is an extremely complex process,* and, second, it seems conceptually more

---

*The work by Kafura and Canning on multiple resources is almost the only foray into this area, other than cost estimation models such as COCOMO[24] and SOFTCOST.[203]

straightforward to start from a simple foundation and introduce complications only as they become necessary. Hence, this chapter deals with
the simple uni-dimensional model, with the following chapter introducing additional factors leading to the construction of a more sophisticated
multi-dimensional model. These two chapters mirror what actually happens during modelling: the initial development of simple models which are
evaluated and then modified until they sufficiently resemble reality.

6.2   Problem identification

The problem is one of controlling the software design process in order to
produce software systems exhibiting the following quality factors: implementability, reliability, and maintainability.

Such quality problems have been exercising researchers for a considerable number of years.[25, 97, 98, 153, 195] Design may be conceived of as a
process of selecting between alternatives, with the objective of providing
an abstract solution* for a given specification or problem. Indeed, if no alternatives exist, then the process is a mechanical one offering no prospect
of improvement. In order to avoid being an entirely stochastic process,
selection must be made on the basis of evaluation criteria. Our objective,
then, is to seek to provide software engineers with a means of discriminating between alternative designs in order to improve the software quality
factors listed above. Furthermore, we wish the design evaluation criteria
to be quantitative.

Although being able to contrast designs is fundamental, this assumes
that one has a repertoire to draw from. In many cases the starting point
may well be a single design, in which case we wish not only to be able to
contrast designs, but also to pin-point weaknesses within a design. This
facilitates the generation of new — and hopefully improved — designs.

Such objectives raise the question as to the relationship between this
research and the various design methodologies that are emerging, such as
object-oriented design.[25] It is our view that the use of metrics as quantitative criteria with which to evaluate software designs is complementary
to methodology because, although a methodology may restrict the search
space for candidate designs considerably, no methodology of which we are
aware restricts the space to a single design† — certainly not for non-

Unfortunately, some of these seem to perform poorly, other than upon their own
databases.[139, 39]

*The solution is abstract in the sense that it is not executable. Were there to exist
a suitable target machine upon which it could run, then, of course, the design would be
an implementation.

†One of the author's experiences of teaching even highly prescriptive methods such
as JSP[97] still supports this proposition. Students were still able to generate surprisingly
diverse solutions, particularly with respect to logical input data structures and whether
to employ a backtracking strategy or not.

trivial problems. The other key difference in approaches is that even when a methodology provides explicit evaluation criteria, as in the case of Structured Design,[142, 194] these tend to be qualitative and, therefore, not amenable to automation.

Finally, it must be stressed that our goal is emphatically not to be able to predict any of the above quality factors from a given design accurately. Accurate prediction requires a far deeper understanding of software engineering processes than we possess at present.[184] Nor is it a likely outcome from a comparatively simple, uni-dimensional model.

6.3 An informal model

The first issue to address is, what aspects of a design should be included in our embryonic model? Work by other researchers, for example Henry,[82] Kafura and Reddy,[104] and Rombach and Basili,[165] suggests that structural, or architectural, aspects of a design are an important determinant of the software quality factors that we are interested in. System architecture also yields the benefit of being available early on in the design phase, thus allowing more scope for strategic decision making, since few resources are yet committed. For the same reason, backtracking and reworking of designs is comparatively cheap.

Our goal imposes the constraint that the metrics must be available at design time.* Thus, we restrict ourselves to the following information:

- modules;
- the calling structure;
- the module interfaces (i.e. the data objects that each module imports and exports);
- global data structure references.

The next problem is to decide what aspects of system architecture to capture. All three quality factors have a software engineering perspective in that they involve the software engineer in work — either to develop, repair or modify the software. Informally, our model is that these tasks are easier to perform the more localized they are. Taking a module as the fundamental unit, flows of information between modules are the means whereby one module may impact another module. If there is the possibility of an information flow, the software engineer must examine additional modules and the task becomes increasingly global in nature. Thus, the fewer connections that exist between a module and other modules the easier it is to

---

*This is an important restriction — one where metrologists allow themselves the luxury of near-perfect foresight — the resulting metrics cannot be integrated into software engineering processes without extreme difficulty. Henry and Kafura's Information Flow metric[82] provides the classic example where their design metric requires LOC as one of its inputs. Similarly, COCOMO[24] requires an estimate of LOC very early on in the software life-cycle.

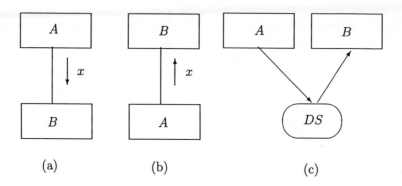

FIG. 6.1. Example information flows between modules A and B.

implement and maintain, and the fewer errors it contains. This provides a justification for treating three software quality factors in one model — that there is a unifying process of comprehension by the software engineer.* Such a model is in line with current developments in design methodology and preferred system architectures.[4, 25, 142, 152, 220]

As already stated, our intention is the development of a uni-dimensional model. However, we did not feel it entirely appropriate to ignore the application domain. Thus there is also the background problem of establishing the extent to which this model is applicable. Consequently, specific application domains are identified. The empirical validation applies the model to interactive systems and real-time embedded systems.

6.4   A formal model

6.4.1   *Definitions*

In order to achieve the goal of aiding software engineers to select suitable designs, the extremely informal model described above must be crystalized into something more specific. The following definitions are therefore introduced.

A module is an executable unit of software that may be called by name, returns execution to the caller after elaboration, and is identified by the system architecture. Information flows between modules either by means of parameters (Figure 6.1(a) and (b)) or via a global data structure (Figure 6.1(c)). A global data structure is any variable that is shared between more than one module, and it may be permanent, such as a file, or temporary, such as an array.

---

*Hindsight would suggest that combining several quality factors into a single model leads to problems, particularly where trade-offs exist, for example development effort could be reduced at the expense of reliability. These problems are enlarged upon towards the end of this chapter.

From these basic definitions, the fan-in fi and fan-out fo of a module may be derived, where fi is the number of information flows terminating at a module and fo is the number of flows emanating from a module. Since our model is concerned only with the number of connected modules, duplicate flows are ignored. These counts are then combined to give an information flow metric $if4$, which, for a module m, is calculated as follows:

$$if4 = (fi * fo)^2 \qquad (6.1)$$

fi is multiplied by fo because it gives the number of unique information paths through a module. This is then raised to the power of two in order to differentiate between architectures where information flows are evenly distributed among the modules, and those architectures that exhibit a clustering of flows around a small number of modules.* Despite the seeming arbitrary nature of a power law of two the approach is in line with Belady and Evangelisti's[21] method for partitioning systems. It is also similar in formulation to the Henry and Kafura metric.[82] In order to contrast complete systems we have used a system metric:

$$if4 = \sum_{m=1}^{n} if4_m \qquad (6.2)$$

where n is the number of modules.

Although this idea is indebted to the pioneering research of Sallie Henry and Denis Kafura,[82] our definitions of information flow are substantially modified, thereby eliminating many of anomalies contained in their original metric and underlying model. These anomalies are described both in Chapter 3 and elsewhere.[112, 181, 90]

6.4.2 An algebraic model specification

Our approach to a more precise description is the use of algebras, sometimes known as *axiomatic specifications*.[72, 125]

We must state the desired characteristics of our measure formally as a set of model invariants. To do this we employ the tailored axiomatic approach outlined in the preceding chapter. Once this has been accomplished we can set about the task of investigating whether there exist inputs which result in violations of the model invariants.

In order to develop an algebra to formally specify a model it is first necessary to consider the constructor operations,[68] bearing in mind that not all feasible concatenations will yield meaningful system architectures. For

---

*The value of the quadratic term has been questioned since most empirical work deals only with weak orderings. It is significant, however, when working at the system level, since the metric sums across modules.

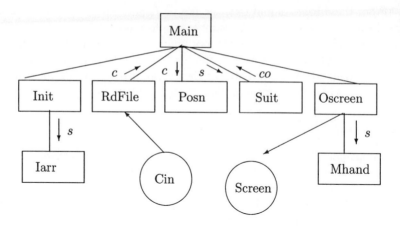

FIG. 6.2. Example system architecture.

example, a flow between two data structures has no meaning in our model — a data structure must be accessed by a module. Thus, we commence with a grammar for our representation language of system architectures. Since the central issue of our model is information flow connection between modules, a directed graph is a convenient tool. We distinguish between two types of nodes: modules and global data structures. The edges show flow of information, either from one module to another as parameters, or between a module and a data structure indicating update or retrieval from the data structure by the module.

Figure 6.2 presents an example of a system architecture which can be represented as the graph shown in Figure 6.3, where a black circle represents a global data structure while a white circle represents a module. From Figure 6.2 we observe that there is no flow of information, either via parameters or via data structures, between the module *Init* and the rest of the system, hence the graph in Figure 6.3 is not connected. Similarly, the modules *Oscreen* and *Mhand* comprise an isolated sub-system represented as another sub-graph. There is, however, a link from *Oscreen* to *Mhand* because *Mhand* imports the parameter s. In reality one might have doubts concerning the utility of a system comprising three entirely independent subsystems, but that is an issue beyond the scope of the present discussion. It is also noteworthy that there are no module-to-module links via *Cin* or *Screen*, the two global data structures, because no module writes to *Cin* and no module reads from *Screen*. Again, this is a rather improbable state of affairs. The edges are not identified, as our concern is only whether a flow exists or not. Since it is a directed graph, the existence of a flow from one module to another does not imply a reverse flow, unless explicitly

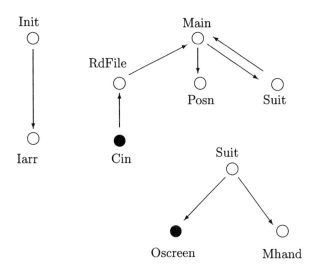

FIG. 6.3. Graph representation of the system architecture.

identified, as in the case of *Main* and *Suit*.

There are certain restrictions upon the building of a graph to describe system architecture. First, to avoid any possibility of ambiguity, nodes (either modules or global data structures) must have unique names. Second, an edge must link two nodes. We avoid, at least at this stage, the issue of recursion and further stipulate that an edge cannot link a node to itself. Finally, an edge may not link two data structure nodes.

This approach yields the advantage of simplicity since we only have two types of object to deal with: nodes and edges. Consequently, there will be two constructor operations:*

> *an*
>
> *ae*

where *an* is the add node constructor and *ae* is the add edge constructor. These will have the following signatures:

> $an : graph \times nodetype \times name \qquad \rightarrow graph \cup \{error\}$
> $ae : graph \times name \times name \qquad\; \rightarrow graph \cup \{error\}$

Note that since the graph is directed, the flow will be from the first node (i.e. the second argument) to the second node (i.e. the third argument) of the *ae* operation. Unfortunately, these operations have one undesirable property for constructors: they are not deterministic because we cannot predict *a priori* whether the constructor operation will succeed, or whether it will

---

*The full specification is given in the appendix.

yield an illegal structure and therefore result in an error being returned. To resolve this problem, two further constructor operations are required which will be deterministic; we will call these *cn* (concatenate-n) and *ce* (concatenate-e). They are referred to as internal operations — instead of external operations — because they are only present to facilitate the formal specification process.

We now specify algebraically the construction of meaningful system structures in terms of graphs as:

types
$$graph$$
$$nodetype = (module, globalds)$$
$$name = string$$

vars
$$S_1, S_2 : graph$$
$$t_1, t_2 : nodetype$$
$$n_1, n_2, n_3, n_4 : name$$

external operations

$an : graph \times nodetype \times name$	$\rightarrow graph \cup \{error\}$
$ae : graph \times name \times name$	$\rightarrow graph \cup \{error\}$

internal operations

$cn : graph \times nodetype \times name$	$\rightarrow graph$
$ce : graph \times name \times name$	$\rightarrow graph$
$new :$	$\rightarrow graph$
$exists : graph \times name$	$\rightarrow boolean$
$linked : graph \times name \times name$	$\rightarrow boolean$
$isamod : graph \times name$	$\rightarrow boolean$
$isads : graph \times name$	$\rightarrow boolean$

Apart from *ce* and *cn*, five other internal operations are introduced: *new* is required to enable an initial state to be defined for the graph (i.e. an empty system architecture), and to detect a boundary condition for the recursive application of other operations; *exists, linked, isamod,* and *isads* facilitate the checking for error conditions when building system architectures. More specifically, *exists* tests whether a named node exists in the graph, and *linked* whether there is an edge leading from the first to the second node. The operations *isamod* and *isads* check the type of a named node. Meaningful, and therefore allowable, concatenations are now defined by the following equations:

$$an(S_1, t_1, n_1) = \text{if } exists(S_1, n_1)$$
$$\text{then}\{error\}$$
$$\text{else } cn(S_1, t_1, n_1)$$

$$ae(S_1, n_1, n_2) \quad = \quad \text{if } exists(S_1, n_1) \land$$
$$exists(S_1, n_2) \land$$
$$\neg linked(S_1, n_1, n_2) \land$$
$$n_1 \neq n_2 \land$$
$$(isamod(S_1, n_1)$$
$$\lor isamod(S_1, n_2))$$
$$\text{then } ce(S_1, t_1, n_1)$$
$$\text{else} \{error\}$$

$$exists(new, n_1) \quad = \quad \text{false}$$
$$exists(cn(S_1, t_1, n_2), n_1) \quad = \quad \text{if } n_1 = n_2$$
$$\text{then true}$$
$$\text{else } exists(S_1, n_1)$$
$$exists(ce(S_1, n_2, n_3), n_1) \quad = \quad \text{if } n_1 = n_2 \lor n_1 = n_3$$
$$\text{then true}$$
$$\text{else } exists(S_1, n_1)$$

$$linked(new, n_1, n_2) \quad = \quad \text{false}$$
$$linked(ce(S_1, n_3, n_4), n_1, n_2) = \quad \text{if } n_3 = n_1 \land n_4 = n_2$$
$$\text{then true}$$
$$\text{else } linked(S_1, n_1, n_2)$$
$$linked(cn(S_1, t_1, n_3), n_1, n_2) = \quad linked(S_1, n_1, n_2)$$

$$isamod(new, n_1) \quad = \quad \text{false}$$
$$isamod(cn(S_1, t_1, n_2), n_1) \quad = \quad \text{if } n_1 = n_2 \land t_1 = module$$
$$\text{then true}$$
$$\text{else } isamod(S_1, n_1)$$
$$isamod(ce(S_1, n_2, n_3), n_1) \quad = \quad isamod(S_1, n_1)$$

$$isads(new, n_1) \quad = \quad \text{false}$$
$$isads(cn(S_1, t_1, n_2), n_1) \quad = \quad \text{if } n_1 = n_12 \land t_1 = globalds$$
$$\text{then true}$$
$$\text{else } isads(S_1, n_1)$$
$$isads(ce(S_1, n_2, n_3), n_1) \quad = \quad isads(S_1, n_1)$$

Note that the fact that *isads* is false does not imply *isamod* is true, or *vice versa*, since both will return false if the node n_1 does not exist. Therefore, both these internal operations are required.

The above is a formal specification of which graphs may be constructed to represent valid system architectures. So, part of the architecture given in Figure 6.2 and Figure 6.3 (the sub-system incorporating *Oscreen*, *Mhand* and the data structure *Screen*) may be described as the following sequence of concatenation* operations:

new

an(new,module,output-screen)

am(an(new,module,output-screen),module,make-hand)

an(an(an(new,module,output-screen),module,make-hand),
global-data-structure,screen)

ae(an(an(an(new,module,output-screen),module,make-hand),
global-data-structure,screen),output-screen,screen)

ae(ae(an(an(an(new,module,output-screen),module,make-hand),
global-data-structure,screen),output-screen,
screen),output-screen,make-hand)

Although this may appear rather arcane, it is merely the successive application of three *an* and two *ae* operations to a *new* graph. Using this technique any legal system architecture can be described unambiguously.

Using the same algebraic approach the *if4* measures can be formally defined. Two additional external operations are introduced:

$$if4 : graph \qquad\qquad \rightarrow nat$$
$$if4_m : graph \times name \qquad \rightarrow nat \cup \{error\}$$

where *nat* is the set of natural numbers. The *if4* operation returns the information flow measure for the entire system and is deterministic. The $if4_m$ operation returns the information flow measure for the module named, and is not deterministic: the name may refer to a node that is either not a module or that is not present within the system.

if4 is defined as being the sum of applying $if4_m$ to every node in the graph that is of the type *module*. In order to specify this algebraically, we search destructively through the graph, processing every node that is a module until the graph is empty. This creates one problem (if we are to preserve the strictly functional style of the algebra), in that the complete graph is needed to determine all information flows for each module, because each module may be linked to any other, or indeed, every other node in the system. Hence we introduce yet another internal operation, *if4int*, which has two arguments: the complete system and the system remaining to be searched.

$$if4int : graph \times graph \qquad\qquad \rightarrow nat$$

---

*One of the properties of our model is that the order of concatenations is immaterial, other than that nodes must precede the introduction of connecting edges. A proof will be provided later in the chapter.

This gives:

$$if4(S_1) \qquad\qquad = \qquad if4int(S_1, S_1)$$

$$if4int(S_1, new) = 0$$
$$if4int(S_1, cn(S_2, t_1, n_1)) = \text{if } t_1 = module$$
$$\text{then } if4_m(S_1, n_1) + if4int(S_1, S_2)$$
$$\text{else } if4(S_1, S_2)$$
$$if4int(S_1, ce(S_2, n_1, n_2)) = if4(S_1, S_2)$$

We now address the problem of defining $if4_m$, the information flow measure for a specific module. By now it will come as little surprise to the reader that the following internal operations must be added to the specification!

$$faninl : graph \times name \qquad\qquad \rightarrow nat$$
$$fanoutl : graph \times name \qquad\qquad \rightarrow nat$$
$$faning : graph \times graph \times name \qquad \rightarrow nat$$
$$fanoutg : graph \times graph \times name \qquad \rightarrow nat$$

Each of these operations determines the number of local or global information flows into, or out of, the specified module. Local flows are information flows via parameters, while global flows are flows via shared data structures. The operations that count global flows have two graph arguments to deal with the problem of destructive searching — for exactly the same reasons as the previously defined $if4$ operation. These may be combined to define $if4_m$ as:

$$if4_m(S_1, n_1) = \text{if } isamod(S_1, n_1)$$
$$\text{then } sqr((faninl(S_1, n_1) + faning(S_1, S_1, n_1))$$
$$*(fanoutl(S_1, n_1) + fanoutg(S_1, S_1, n_1)))$$
$$\text{else} \{error\}$$

$$faninl(new, n_1) = 0$$
$$faninl(ce(S_1, n_2, n_3), n_1)$$
$$= \text{if } n_3 = n_1 \wedge isamod(n_2)$$
$$\text{then } 1 + faninl(S_1, n_1)$$
$$\text{else } faninl(S_1, n_1)$$
$$faninl(cn(S_1, t_1, n_2), n_1)$$
$$= faninl(S_1, n_1)$$

$$fanoutl(new, n_1) = 0$$
$$fanoutl(ce(S_1, n_2, n_3), n_1)$$
$$= \text{if } n_2 = n_1 \wedge isamod(n_3)$$
$$\text{then } 1 + fanoutl(S_1, n_1)$$
$$\text{else } fanoutl(S_1, n_1)$$
$$fanoutl(cn(S_1, t_1, n_2), n_1)$$
$$= fanout(S_1, n_1)$$

$$faning(S_1, new, n_1) \;=\; 0$$
$$faning(S_1, concate(S_2, n_2, n_3), n_1)$$
$$\qquad = \; \text{if } n_3 = n_1 \wedge isads(n_2)$$
$$\qquad\qquad \text{then } ctglobalsin(S_1, S_2, n_1, n_2) + faning(S_1, S_2, n_1$$
$$\qquad\qquad \text{else } faning(S_1, S_2, n_1)$$
$$faning(S_1, concatn(S_2, t_1, n_2), n_1)$$
$$\qquad = \; faning(S_1, S_2, n_1)$$

$$fanoutg(S_1, new, n_1) = \; 0$$
$$fanoutg(S_1, concate(S_2, n_2, n_3), n_1)$$
$$\qquad = \; \text{if } n_3 = n_1 \wedge isads(n_2)$$
$$\qquad\qquad \text{then }$$
$$\qquad\qquad ctglobalsout(S_1, S_2, n_1, n_2) + fanoutg(S_1, S_2, n_1)$$
$$\qquad\qquad \text{else } fanoutg(S_1, S_2, n_1)$$
$$fanoutg(S_1, concatn(S_2, t_1, n_2), n_1)$$
$$\qquad = \; fanoutg(S_1, S_2, n_1)$$

In order to determine the number of global flows into module n_1 via global data structure n_2 the entire graph S_1 must be searched using $ctglobalsin$.

$$ctglobalsin : graph \times graph \times name \times name \;\;\rightarrow nat$$

To count global flows out of module n_1 via global data structure n_2 we have:

$$ctglobalsout : graph \times graph \times name \times name \;\rightarrow nat$$

These are defined as:

$$ctglobalsin(S_1, new, n_1, n_2) \;=\; \quad 0$$
$$ctglobalsin(S_1, ce(S_2, n_3, n_4), n_1, n_2)$$
$$\qquad = \; \text{if } n_4 = n_2 \wedge isamod(n_3) \wedge n_3 \neq n_1$$
$$\qquad\qquad \text{then } 1 + ctglobalsin(S_1, S_2, n_1, n_2)$$
$$\qquad\qquad \text{else} ctglobalsin(S_1, S_2, n_1, n_2)$$
$$ctglobalsin(S_1, cn(S_2, t_1, n_3), n_1, n_2)$$
$$\qquad = \; ctglobalsin(S_1, S_2, n_1, n_2)$$

$$ctglobalsout(S_1, new, n_1, n_2) = \quad 0$$
$$ctglobalsout(S_1, ce(S_2, n_3, n_4), n_1, n_2)$$
$$\qquad = \; \text{if } n_3 = n_2 \wedge isamod(n_4) \wedge n_4 \neq n_1$$
$$\qquad\qquad \text{then } 1 + ctglobalsout(S_1, S_2, n_1, n_2)$$
$$\qquad\qquad \text{else } ctglobalsout(S_1, S_2, n_1, n_2)$$
$$ctglobalsout(S_1, cn(S_2, t_1, n_3), n_1, n_2)$$
$$\qquad = \; ctglobalsout(S_1, S_2, n_1, n_2)$$

This, then, completes the algebraic definition of the model and the information flow metrics. It yields the advantage of being unambiguous — particularly with respect to the validity of structures — and provides the apparatus for reasoning about, and evaluating, the model. Formal evaluation is made easier when combined with the next step, which is to state the properties that we desire of our model as a set of model invariants or axioms. To do this we adopt the tailored, three-layer approach set out in the preceding chapter.

6.4.3 *Axioms of desired model behaviour*

The first set of axioms for the model are those that are fundamental to all measurement, as described in the preceding chapter. Since these do not vary with the model we will postpone re-rehearsing them until the next section on theoretical evaluation.

Regarding the second class of axioms, these are dependent upon our choice of measurement scale. In this instance the relationships identified within the model are concerned with input and output variable ranks which, in turn, suggests that weak ordering will be sufficient for our purposes. This implies ordinal measurement. The axioms are those of transitivity of the $<$ and $>$ relations and symmetry, reflexivity, and transitivity of the equivalence relation. Further discussion is given Krantz *et al.*,[118] Kyburg,[119] and Melton *et al.*[137]

The third class of axioms are those that relate to the specific model underlying the measure in question. Again, it is possible to provide categories under which axioms may be selected. These are:

- resolution;
- empirically meaningless structures;
- model invariants.

No further axioms concerning measurement resolution are required beyond the axiom which states that the measure must be capable of discrimination, and the fourth axiom, which states that there must exist at least two system architectures that will be assigned to the same equivalence class.

As regards the second category; the axiomatization of the concatenation operations *cn* and *ce* formally define all legal or meaningful system architectures. Thus, no further axioms are required.

The third category of axioms are those properties specific to this model which we believe are important properties and must therefore remain invariant.

Axiom 6.7 *Concatenating an additional module to the system architecture cannot decrease the if4* measure:*

$$\forall S_1 \in graph; m_1 \in node \bullet isamod(m_1) \wedge |S_1| \leq |cn(S_1, module, m_1)|$$

Axiom 6.8 *Concatenating an additional data structure to the system architecture will not change the if4 measure:*

**if4 is being used as shorthand for development effort, maintainability, and unreliability.

$\forall S_1 \in graph; ds_1 \in node\bullet$
$\qquad isads(ds_1) \wedge |S_1| = |cn(S_1, globalds, ds_1)|$

Axiom 6.9 *Concatenating an additional local information flow to the system architecture must increase the if4 measure:*

$\forall S_1 \in graph; m_1, m_2 \in node\bullet$
$\qquad isamod(m_1) \wedge isamod(m_2) \wedge m_1 \neq m_2 \wedge$
$\qquad |S_1| < |ce(S_1, m_1, m_2)| \wedge |S_1| < |ce(S_1, m_2, m_1)|$

Axiom 6.10 *Concatenating an additional global information flow to the system architecture must increase the if4 measure.*

There is a slight difficulty in stating this invariant formally because not all edges leading to or from data structures create global flows: a structure remains a sink or source (e.g. no flow exists if ten modules update a global data structure but no module retrieves from it — admittedly a rather bizarre situation!):

$\forall S_1 \in graph; m_1, ds_1 \in node\bullet$
$\qquad \exists m_2 \in node\bullet$
$\qquad\qquad isamod(m_1) \wedge isamod(m_2) \wedge m_1 \neq m_2 \wedge isads(ds_1) \wedge$
$\qquad\qquad linked(S_1, ds_1, m_2) \wedge |S_1| < |ce(S_1, m_1, ds_1)|$

$\forall S_1 \in graph; m_1, ds_1 \in node\bullet$
$\qquad \exists m_2 \in node\bullet$
$\qquad\qquad isamod(m_1) \wedge isamod(m_2) \wedge m_1 \neq m_2 \wedge isads(ds_1) \wedge$
$\qquad\qquad linked(S_1, m_2, ds_1) \wedge |S_1| < |ce(S_1, ds_1, m_1)|$

Axiom 6.11 *The if4 measures are not a monotonic function of counts of system components (i.e. modules, global data structures and flows):*

$\exists S_1, S_2 \in graph\bullet$
$\qquad nmods(S_1) > nmods(S_2) \wedge |S_1| < |S_2|$

$\exists S_1, S_2 \in graph\bullet$
$\qquad nds(S_1) > nds(S_2) \wedge |S_1| < |S_2|$

$\exists S_1, S_2 \in graph\bullet$
$\qquad nfl(S_1) > nfl(S_2) \wedge |S_1| < |S_2|$

where *nmods* is a function that returns the number of modules contained in a system architecture, *nds* is a function that returns the number of global data structures contained in a system architecture, and *nfl* is a function that returns the number of local and global information flows contained in a system architecture.

One problem that we noted in our critique of Henry and Kafura's metric[82] was the way in which their model behaved with respect to component re-use. This leads to the next axiom.

Axiom 6.12 *A system reusing components must not have a greater if4 measure than a similar system duplicating the component:*

$\forall R \in graph;\, A, B, C, D \in node\bullet$
$\quad isamod(A) \land isamod(B) \land isamod(C) \land$
$\quad isamod(D) \land C = D \land |ce(S, B, C)| \leq |ce(cn(S, module, D), C, D)|$

$\forall R \in graph;\, A, B, C, D \in node\bullet$
$\quad isamod(A) \land isamod(B) \land isamod(C) \land isamod(D) \land$
$\quad C = D \land |ce(S, C, B)| \leq |ce(cn(S, module, D), D, C)|$

Two contrasting, but functionally similar, structures can be defined as:

S = ce(cn(cn(cn(R,module,A),module,B),module,C),A,C)

Similarly, we have the inverse:

S = ce(cn(cn(cn(R,module,A),module,B),module,C),C,A)

In the following section we will assess the extent to which our model conforms to these axioms. It is worth pointing out that the notation that we use is rather poor, for example it contains rather a large number of brackets. The reason for this is that it has been designed specifically to be processed by tools such as algebraic specification provers.

6.5   Theoretical model behaviour

The necessary groundwork has now been set up to start a theoretical evaluation of the model of software design. Theoretical evaluation precedes empirical evaluation because convincing empirical investigations are usually lengthy and energy-consuming enterprises. It is therefore appropriate to satisfy ourselves that the model is internally consistent and satisfies the various criteria that are set as axioms. We should like to make it clear that there is no suggestion, however, that theoretical analysis should replace empirical evaluation totally.

First, we will consider those properties that are fundamental to all measurement, as described in the preceding chapter.

Axiom 6.1 *It must be possible to describe, even if not formally, the rules governing the measurement. This is satisfied by the algebraic definition of if4.**

Axiom 6.2 *The measure must generate at least two equivalence classes.*

Here, it is necessary to demonstrate that two system architectures exist, such that when the operation $if4$ is applied they yield different results. The

---

*Furthermore this definition has been shown to be fully operational by transforming the algebra into OBJ and executing the program.

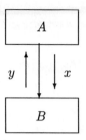

FIG. 6.4. Example system design.

simplest structure is of course the null, or empty, structure. Equations 15
and 16 from the appendix* are:

$$if4\,(new) = if4int(new, new)$$

$$if4int(new, new) = 0$$

It now only remains to show that an architecture exists for which $if4$ does
not return zero. To do this we will build a system with two modules, A
and B, and information flows between them. This is shown in Figure 6.4
The necessary constructors are:

$$ce(ce(cn(cn(new, module, A), module, B), A, B), B, A)$$

so the expression to evaluate is:

$$if4(ce(ce(cn(cn(new, module, A), module, B), A, B)), B, A)$$

which by equation 15 is

$$if4int(ce(ce(cn(cn(concatn(new, module, A), module, B), A, B), B, A)),$$
$$(ce(ce(cn(cn(new, module, A), module, B), A, B), B, A))$$

which is

$$if4int(ce(ce(cn(cn(new, module, A), module, B), A, B), B, A)),$$
$$(cn(cn(new, module, A), module, B))$$

Instantiating into equation 17 for $t1$ being equal to $module$ gives:

$$if4int(ce(ce(cn(cn(new, module, A), module, B), A, B), B, A)),$$
$$if4m(sqr(ce(ce(cn(cn(new, module, A), module, B), A, B), B, A), B))$$
$$+(cn(new, module, A)))$$

---

*All single equation numbers refer to the equations in the full specification detailed
in the appendix.

Instantiating into equation 19 *isamod* will return true for B yielding:*

$if4int(ce(ce(cn(cn(new, module, A), module, B), A, B), B, A)),$
$sqr(((faninl(ce(ce(cn(cn(new, module, A), module, B), A, B), B, A), B)$
$+(faning(ce(ce(cn(cn(new, module, A), module, B), A, B), B, A), B))$
$*((fanoutl(ce(ce(cn(cn(new, module, A), module, B), A, B), B, A), B)$
$+(fanoutg(ce(ce(cn(cn(new, module, A), module, B), A, B), B, A), B))$
$+(cn(new, module, A))))$

Evaluating the *faning* and *fanoutg* terms by applying equations 26–31 we obtain zero in each case, since there is no node for which *isads* returns true and therefore the *then* part of equations 27 and 30 are never used when rewriting. Consequently, the argument S_2 must reduce to the empty structure and must yield zero by equations 26 and 29.

faninl and *fanoutl* are a little more complex so we show each stage in the rewriting process.

$faninl(ce(ce(cn(cn(new, module, A), module, B), A, B), B, A), B)$

By instantiating into equation 21 $n_3 \neq n_1$:

$faninl(ce(cn(cn(new, module, A), module, B), A, B), B)$

Again we apply equation 21 this time with $n_3 = n_1$. This is followed by the application of equation 22 twice and equation 20

$1 + faninl(cn(cn(new, module, A), module, B), B)$

$1 + faninl(cn(new, module, A), B)$

$1 + faninl(new), B)$

$1 + 0$

Similarly, with *fanoutl* and equations 23, – 25 we obtain:

$fanoutl(ce(ce(cn(cn(new, module, A), module, B), A, B), B, A), B)$

Substituting back into the preceding expression and using equation 17 we now have:

$sqr(((1 + 0) * (1 + 0))) + if4int(ce(ce(cn(cn(new, module, A),$
$module, B), A, B), B, A), (cn(new, module, A)))$

$1 + if4_m(ce(ce(cn(cn(new, module, A), module, B), A, B), B, A), A)$
$+if4int(ce(ce(cn(cn(new, module, A), module, B), A, B), B, A), new)$

$if4_m$ for module A will behave as for module B yielding

$sqr(((1 + 0) * (1 + 0)))$

---

*Even we realize that the expression that follows is hugely complex. It is a very potent argument for using some sort of tool support such as an automatic rewrite tool.

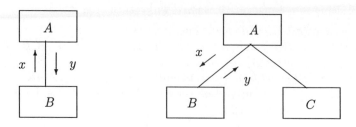

FIG. 6.5. Two designs with equivalent *if4* values.

which is 1. Our overall expression for *if4* now becomes:

$$1 + 1 + if4int(ce(ce(cn(cn(new, module, A), module, B), A, B), B, A), new)$$

which is 2.

As the rewrite sequence now terminates we have a result of applying the *if4* operation to the system of two, which is clearly distinct from zero so we are able to satisfy the second axiom.

As will be all too evident to the reader, constructing this style of proof is both lengthy and tedious. For subsequent axioms only the outline of a proof is given and the reader is referred to Shepperd.[183]

Axiom 6.3 *An equality relation is required.*

No proof is presented as the relation is axiomatic to our algebraic system, along with propositional logic and natural numbers.

Axiom 6.4 *There must exist two or more structures that will be assigned to the same equivalence class.*

To satisfy this axiom, all that is required is to find two different design structures that yield the same measurement. Two such structures are shown in Figure 6.5. The proofs are omitted because they are both intuitively obvious and somewhat tedious.*

Axiom 6.5 *The metric must not produce anomalies, that is, the metric must preserve empirical orderings.*

There are two aspects to this axiom. The first is the mapping of the measurement function and the second is the definition of relations upon the measurement system. Unfortunately, as has been indicated previously, the first part of the axiom is an open problem due to the absence of generally

---

*For the benefit of the reader who is of either a masochistic or sceptical disposition, the proof is based upon the observation that the *fanin* and *fanout* terms only potentially increment for *ce* operations. Thus, no number of *cn* operations (i.e. addition of modules or global data structures) will impact the *fanin* or *fanout* terms and hence $if4_m$ and *if4*. Extending this argument it can be shown by induction that there in fact exist an infinite number of structures for each equivalence class.

agreed empirical relations. Hence, the first part of the proof of this axiom cannot be discharged; however, since the measurement system is based upon the number system of natural numbers, the existence of equivalent relations in the empirical and measurement systems can be demonstrated.* The proof of this can be found in Krantz et al.[118]

Axiom 6.6 *The Uniqueness Theorem must hold[199] for all permissible transformations for the particular type of scale, that is, there is a homomorphism between the transformed and the measurement structures.*

The underlying question is whether the measurement system is adequate for the type of measurement scale selected. For an ordinal scale the measurement structure must be order preserving for any monotonically increasing transformation function. This is trivially true.[118, 193, 199]

Axiom 6.7 *Concatenating an additional module to the design structure cannot decrease the if4 measure.*

The proof is the corollary for that of Axiom 4, in that if by adding nodes (modules or global data structures) additional members of the same equivalence class are generated, the *if4* measure cannot be decreased.

Axiom 6.8 *Concatenating an additional global data structure to the design structure cannot decrease the if4 measure.*

This holds for the same reason as Axiom 7.

Axiom 6.9 *Concatenating an additional local information flow to the design structure must increase the if4 measure.*

To show that the axiom holds for the model we argue inductively that it is true for the following two structures where the outside *ce* represents the information flow being added to the design:

$$ce(cn(cn(new, module, a), module, b), a, b)$$

$$ce(cn(cn(N, module, a), module, b), a, b)$$

The first structure contains zero flows, to which we add a local information flow. The second structure is the case where the structure n already contains $n + 1$ flows where N is non-negative integer. A full discussion is given in Shepperd,[183] however in brief, it is found that the axiom does not hold for the first structure above as it has an *if4* value of zero, both before and after an information flow is added. This is a significant result because it indicates that Axiom 9 does not hold over our model since adding the edge to the graph to represent the local information flow has not increased the *if4* measure; it remains at zero. The reason for this is not difficult to find.

---

*In practice this axiom only becomes non-trivial when the measurement system is based upon such mathematical exotica as vectors, when it is not at all obvious that the Representation Theorem holds as, for example, in Hansen's modification to the cyclomatic measure.[78]

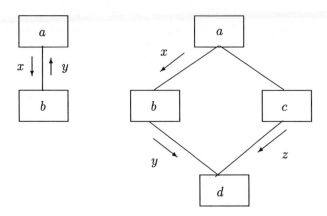

FIG. 6.6. An example where the number of modules is not related to $if4$ values.

The definition of $if4$ involves multiplying the fan-in by the fan-out of each module. Should one term be zero this will propagate through the metric definition giving zero overall.* The significance of this axiom violation will be discussed more fully at the end of the chapter.

Axiom 6.10 *Concatenating an additional global information flow to the design structure must increase the if4 measure.*

This axiom can be violated by presenting the same type of example as for the preceding axiom where adding an additional flow to a module where either the fan-in or fan-out remains zero will not increase the $if4$ measure. Again, the implications will be discussed more fully at the end of this chapter.

Axiom 6.11 *Larger designs in terms of the number of modules may have lower if4 measures than smaller designs.*

This axiom can easily be supported by reference to the two examples below which are depicted in Figure 6.6:

$ce(ce(ce(cn(cn(cn(cn(new, module, a), module, b), module, c),$
$module, d), a, b), c, d), b, d)$

$ce(ce(cn(cn(new, module, a), module, b), a, b), b, a)$

The first design has four modules while the second has only two modules, yet it has an $if4$ of 2 as opposed to zero.

---

*This difficulty is also to encountered with Kafura and Henry's original information flow metric.[103]

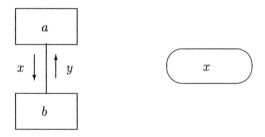

FIG. 6.7. An example where the number of data structures is not related to $if4$ values.

Axiom 6.12 *Larger designs in terms of the number of data structures may have lower $if4$ measures than smaller designs.*

This axiom is demonstrated by reference to the two examples below and is depicted in Figure 6.7:

$$cn(new, globalds, x)$$

$$ce(ce(cn(cn(new, module, a), module, b), a, b), b, a)$$

The first design contains one data structure but has no flows and therefore $if4$ is zero. The second design is the same as for the preceding axiom, it has no data structures, yet $if4$ is two.

Axiom 6.13 *Larger designs in terms of the number of information flows (both local and global) may have lower $if4$ measures than smaller designs.*

This axiom is demonstrated by reference to the two examples used in the discussion relating to Axiom 11. The first design contains three flows, while the second design has two flows; yet the $if4$ measure for the second example is the greater of the two. There are two reasons why this can occur. First, there is the impact of a zero term in a module fan-in or fan-out, as has already been illustrated with respect to Axiom 9. This is the factor at work in this case. Second, the quadratic term will penalize distributions of flows that exhibit clustering tendencies.

Axiom 6.14 *Module reuse must not be penalized in comparison to component duplication.*

Clearly, the issues at stake are the number of reuses and the flows from the module, independent of the reuse interface.

Unfortunately, as with the original Henry and Kafura metric,[81] this axiom does not hold for all cases. This may be demonstrated by a simple example. Referring back to Figure 6.3, the two architectures described differ only in that the first architecture reuses module C, that is, both modules A and B invoke module B; however, in the second architecture module B

Table 6.1 *Comparison of reuse strategies between two architectures*

Architecture 1				Architecture 2			
Module	Fan-in	Fan-out	$if4_m$	Module	Fan-in	Fan-out	$if4_m$
A	1	1	1	A	1	1	1
B	1	1	1	B	1	1	1
C	2	2	16	C	1	1	1
				D	1	1	1
$if4 = 18$				$if4 = 4$			

uses a duplicate of module C, that is, module D. Table 6.1 shows the *if4* values by module to arrive at an overall comparison of the two architectures. From the above, it can be clearly seen that the architecture that reuses a module has a higher overall *if4* value than the architecture that duplicates a module. Not only does this violate generally accepted good software engineering practice, it also violates our axiom. More serious still is the implication that the model of system architecture and information flow is inadequate because it does not properly capture the concept of separate instantiations of the same module that occur whenever a module is invoked from different parts of a system architecture. In particular, it suggests that our definition of information flow is insufficiently broad in scope to deal with module reuse. This is an important finding because it requires us to rethink certain aspects of the model that underlies the metric.

Three potential problems have been identified from the theoretical analysis of the *if4* metric. First, the introduction of an additional local information flow into a design does not always result in an increase in the metric value, the reason for this being the effect of zero flows into or out of a module. The second problem is similar to this: that the addition of a global flow does not always lead to an increase in *if4*. The third problem is possibly more serious, in that software reuse is penalized as compared with module duplication. The reason for this is that the metric does not distinguish between memoryless or deterministic modules and those whose effect depends upon the previous calling history. Some suggested solutions to these problems will be presented in the concluding section of this chapter.

6.6   An empirical analysis

As we have continually stated in this book theoretical evaluation by itself is not enough. The next step is to carry out some empirical evaluation. The aim of this chapter is to describe this evaluation. It represents the minimum level of statistics and experimental design that we feel should be employed for this form of metrics valdiation.

Two empirical studies were carried out. Their aim was to validate the model of information flow against the stated goal: of aiding the designer to select appropriate architectures to maximize the software quality factors of implementability, reliability, and maintainability.

The first study addressed the software quality factor of development effort. Data was used from 13 software teams, where each team comprised three or four second-year students from the BSc Computer Science course at Wolverhampton University. The students were unaware that an experiment was being conducted. Each team implemented the same problem, thus facilitating comparison between systems. Students were allocated to teams in such a fashion as to minimize differences in ability and background, and this was accomplished by examining past grades in software courses coupled with the judgement of tutors.

Each team was required to produce an adventure game shell which could be customized by the players to meet their own requirements. Despite implementing the same specification, systems varied in size from 14 to 33 modules, and from 313 to 983 executable lines of code (ELOC). The systems were written in Pascal. Development effort was recorded by monitoring computer connect time, and by requesting students to submit a record of effort expended on the software development. Unfortunately, cross-checking revealed the manual records to be extremely unreliable, for instance in several cases computer connect time exceeded total development reported manually. They were therefore discarded.

Error data was also collected but was found to be too sparse to permit meaningful analysis. For the majority of systems no errors were detected. This was probably the result of relatively small-scale systems: none exceeded 1000 lines of executable code. Furthermore, the standard testing that each system was subjected to may have been less demanding than if the software had been used in a 'live' environment.

Although not initially intended, it was necessary to treat the results as weak orders, i.e. place in rank order only, due to the highly skewed distributions of the metrics. As a consequence, all correlation coefficients given are non-parametric Spearman values. Table 6.2 presents the cross-correlations.

Design size was defined as the number of modules, the number of information flows, and the number of information flows normalized by the number of modules. In addition, we also used ELOC, although to constitute a design metric this would have to be estimated. Since ELOC* was intended as a control the assumption of perfect estimating did not seem unreasonable. The Spearman correlation of $r = 0.797$ between development time and $if4$ was statistically significant, there being less than a 1% chance of such a correlation occurring by chance. This relationship is shown in Figure 6.8 as a scatter diagram. By contrast, the size measures

---

*ELOC was used as it smoothed out size discrepancies due to code layout. In general, ELOC was found to be approximately 50% of LOC.

Table 6.2 *Cross correlations for adventure game study*

	Development time	$if4$	Flows	Modifications
$if4$	.797			
Flows	−.389	−.508		
Modifications	−.190	−.229	.268	
ELOC	−.217	−.196	.287	.646

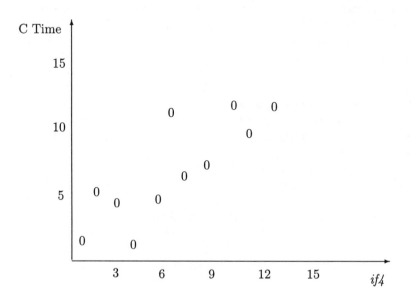

FIG. 6.8. Scatter plot of $if4$ versus connect time (ranks used).

have weak or no correlation with development time. We note parenthetically that the original Henry and Kafura measure had a correlation of $r = 0.434$ with development time, which is statistically insignificant (there being more than a 5% chance of this being a random occurrence). For a more detailed account of the study and analysis of the results the reader is referred to Shepperd[177] or Shepperd.[182]

Size factors do not seem to be significant determinants of development effort but, in contrast, some structural factors are highly related, in particular $if4$. Whether these findings would translate to systems with larger variations in size is unclear. In this study the largest system was three times greater than the smallest. However, if, as stated in our goal, the measures are intended to help the designer select between alternative architectures for the same problem, it is unlikely that there will be a very large variation in size, so this is not necessarily a great stumbling block.

Table 6.3 *An analysis of maintenance judgements*

Max-min	% of judgements
0	10
1	63
2	27
3	0

Where size seems to be of more importance is at an individual component or intra-system level. One system was discarded from the study because of an exceptionally large component, and another had to be re-examined due to a 'super' data structure. This is a disadvantage inherent in a uni-dimensional model, where trade-offs between module size and inter-modular information flows are ignored.* Indeed, taking this point to an extreme, one could construct an 'optimal' system architecture comprising a single module, where all the information flows and interface complexity would be subsumed within the module boundary. However, our understanding of software engineering principles suggests that this would not be good practice!

So far, our discussion has centred on the information flow measure at a system-wide level, but it can be obtained on a module-by-module basis. This is a potentially useful means of identifying problem areas within a design, particularly when coupled with outlier analysis.[184] Thus, the software engineer is aided in the generation of new designs.

A second empirical study was based upon a real-time, aerospace application developed by Lucas Aerospace Ltd. In this study we examined a system comprising 89 separate modules from a real-time control system in order to consider the software quality factor of maintainability.

The four members of staff most closely associated with maintenance work on this project classified each module independently into one of four categories according to the perceived complexity of carrying out a maintenance task on that module. A score of 1 indicated a very simple module, while a score of 4 indicated a highly complex module. This procedure was adopted since it represented the fastest method of obtaining a measure of maintenance problems, and because alternative documentary evidence concerning maintenance costs and traceability to specific modules was unavailable.

Despite initial reservations about subjective evaluations, a strong correspondence was found between the four classifications. The judgement discrepancies are summarized in Table 6.3. It is noteworthy that for almost 75% of the judgements there was either no difference, or a difference

---

*A system architecture comprising a single module will always have zero information flows, regardless of module size.

Table 6.4 *The predictive power of the $if4m$ metric*

	Hi-metric	Lo-metric	Total
Hi-maintenance	14	9	23
Lo-maintenance	9	57	66
Total	23	66	89

of only one between the highest and lowest scores. Also, in no case was a module judged by one member of the maintenance team to be a very simple module to change, and judged as highly complex by another member — such a situation would have led to a discrepancy of three. To obtain an overall picture of maintenance difficulty for each module, the individual subjective judgements were summed to give a total possible score ranging from 4 (trivial) to 16 (highly complex). Actual scores ranged from 4 to 15 with a mean value of 8.7.

The $if4_m$ metric varied from a minimum score of zero to a maximum of 2 924 100, but with a median value of 196, thereby the highly skewed nature of the distribution. A Spearman correlation test was carried out between perceived maintenance complexity and the information flow metric. A correlation coefficient of $r = 0.70$ was obtained which was statistically significant (less than a 1% chance of occurring by chance). In order to provide some basis for comparison, a correlation coefficient of $r = 0.72$ was obtained between the maintenance scores and LOC, and the cross-correlation between LOC and $if4$ was $r = 0.49$, suggesting that $if4$ is more than a mere proxy for size as captured by LOC. Although the traditional LOC measure slightly outperforms $if4$, one must remember that $if4$ is available much earlier in the development and maintenance process. Lastly, this study suggests that there is potential merit in combining an architecture metric, such as $if4$, and a size metric such as LOC, in order to provide better coverage of troublesome modules from a maintenance perspective.

The effectiveness of the design metric as a means of identifying problem modules can be demonstrated as follows: if problem modules are defined to be those that fall into the upper quartile of values for the complexity judgements, then these can be compared with those modules that fall into the upper quartile of the design metric. This indicates the predictive power of the design metric. In this instance the metric would have identified 14 out of 23 of the most troublesome modules, a yield of about 64%. On the other hand, the metric highlights 9 modules as being complex when in fact they have not proved to be so, an error rate of 36%. By contrast, if one were selecting modules at random one would expect a yield of 25% and an error rate of 75%. These results are shown in Table 6.4.

There is an obvious weakness in this investigation. This is the reliance upon the subjective judgement of a small number of individuals. Further

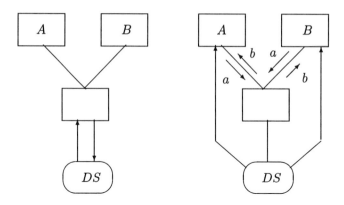

FIG. 6.9. An example of a module with and without memory.

work is required to explore the relationship between perceived complexity from a maintenance change point of view, and actual historical data, such as mean effort per change per module and the probability of a module being impacted in any one maintenance change. This is illustrative of the iterative nature of any software engineering application of software metrics and modelling. Again, it is worth stressing that this chapter is not an attempt to sell the $if4$ metric. We realize that it has some limitations — limitations which are overcome by a metric described in the Chapter 7 — the main aim of this chapter has been to show how our metrics development method can be used to derive a metric; in this case the example we used was the $if4$ metric.

6.7   Evaluation of the uni-dimensional model

To summarize the position so far, three problems have been uncovered by the theoretical analysis of the model   – two of them minor and one more significant. In addition, the empirical studies have raised the problem of component size and, in particular, module size within a system architecture. Each of these areas will be dealt with in turn.

First, the comparatively minor issue of zero terms propagating through the expression to compute $if4$. The consequence of this is that additional local or global flows do not invariably increase the overall $if4$ value. A simple solution to this problem is the addition of one to both the fan-in and fan-out terms as advocated in Ince and Shepperd.[90] Thus the new definition of $if4_m$ becomes:

$$if4_m = ((1 + fanin) * (1 + fanout))^2$$

The solution to the reuse problem is a little more complex. As has already been remarked upon, there is a need to distinguish between module reuse

Table 6.5 *Comparison of reuse strategies between two architectures counting interfaces once*

Architecture 1				Architecture 2			
Module	Fan-in	Fan-out	$if4_m$	Module	Fan-in	Fan-out	$if4_m$
A	1	1	1	A	1	1	1
B	1	1	1	B	1	1	1
C	1	1	1	C	1	1	1
				D	1	1	1
$if4 = 3$				$if4 = 4$			

when behaviour cannot be influenced by previous invocation from other modules, and when this is not the case. The situations can be readily distinguished on the basis of classifying a module either as having a memory or as being memoryless. If a module, or any of its subordinates, writes to a data structure and if any of the same modules reads from the same data structure, then that module is said have a memory.* An example of both types of module is given in Figure 6.9, the first architecture illustrating a reused module with memory. Where reused modules are deemed to be memoryless their interface should only be counted once, rather than once per module invocation. The consequence of this is to be either neutral, or to favour module reuse as required by Axiom 14. Returning to the example used to refute Axiom 14 in Section 6.3 and applying the modified rules described above, a new set of metric values are obtained. As may be seen from Table 6.5 the architecture that reuses rather than duplicates a module now has the lower metric value.†

Turning to the issue of module size raised by the empirical analysis, a solution is more difficult. The fundamental problem is that software architecture is rather complex to model when using only a single dimension or measure. What is really required is a second measure that captures the notion of module size, in addition to module interface complexity in terms of information flows. Chapter 7 proceeds to explore enhancements to the model by means of introducing a second dimension.

To conclude, then, the single dimensional model has some utility, as demonstrated by the two empirical studies, and has been shown to be significantly related to both development effort and maintainability. This is

---

*Strictly speaking, even if these conditions pertain, one can only state that there exists the possibility for modules with memory. However, this may only be resolved by dynamic analysis, which is outside the ambit of the model for reasons that have been discussed previously.

†The concept of memory and memoryless modules may have a secondary application in that reused modules with memory are likely to be lacking in cohesion.[195] This is significant since module cohesion has always proved more difficult to capture than module coupling, see, for example, the discussion in Shepperd and Ince.[187]

despite three theoretical problems that have been uncovered by the application of an axiomatic treatment of an algebraic or formal definition of the model.*

6.8 Summary

This chapter has shown our metric development method in action. It was used to derive and evaluate a metric based on a uni-dimensional model of software design. Once the metric was developed it was subjected to both theoretical and empirical evaluation. Both these evaluations pointed out errors in the metric which were due to its uni-dimensional genesis. The next chapter describes how a more sophisticated metric based on a more realistic model can be generated and evaluated using our method.

*A possible reason why the empirical analysis was broadly supportive, despite the problems highlighted by the theoretical analysis, was that none of the architectures significantly reused modules, coupled with the fact that those designs that were bad were so bad that they tended to overwhelm more marginal features such as the degree of module redundancy!

7

A MULTI-DIMENSIONAL MODEL OF DESIGN

Synopsis

This chapter mirrors the model development process in that it replaces the simpler model of software design described in the preceding chapter with a more sophisticated multi-dimensional model. We demonstrate our metrics development technique in deriving a metric associated with this model. A major conclusion that emerges from the chapter is that if software engineering models are to be useful, then they will require more sophistication than can be achieved by a single input or dimension. In particular, it shows that some of the weaknesses of the model of system architecture described in the preceding chapter may be overcome by extending it to incorporate a notion of module, or design component size. This permits the exploration of trade-offs between inter- and intra-modular information flows. The conclusion is drawn that the techniques employed in this and the preceding chapter enable more sophisticated and useful software models to be developed. However, this must build upon the foundation of theoretically clean and empirically observed relationships. Otherwise, our sophistication is entirely in vain.

7.1 Why multi-dimensional models?

This book has argued that there is support — both theoretical and empirical — for the proposition that a structural metric such as $if4$ can identify potentially problematic architectures and components — typically modules.[90, 182, 180] Clearly, it is of great value to the designer to be able to obtain feedback on design decisions prior to ossifying them into code. There is a danger, however, that lurks behind concentration upon structural measures: the possibility of reducing structural complexity measures merely by adopting very large components.

Unfortunately, a single measure of structure cannot be sensitive to this process. Basili and Rombach[16] make a similar point: they argue that most aspects of software development processes and products are too complex to be captured adequately by a single metric. Consequently, useful models will normally incorporate more than one dimension. Nevertheless, we still wish to assume, subject to the restriction imposed by the objective of providing guidance for the software designer, that all measures must be available at design time.

The remainder of this chapter investigates the various existing metrics for system component size: that is, the full Henry and Kafura information flow metric,[82] the Card and Agresti intra-modular metric,[31] the work by Sampson et al. on formal specification,[167] the deMarco 'Bang' metric,[47] and, finally, Albrecht's function point metric.[2] All of the above are found wanting in at least one respect, so an alternative metric, module 'work', is proposed, based upon the traceability of functional requirements from specification to design. The behavioural properties of the underlying model are analysed by means of the tailored axiomatic approach that we have already described previously. This measure is then applied to empirical data and found to yield useful results and to perform more reliably than the other metrics evaluated. It is suggested that a multi-dimensional model is more effective at identifying problem modules than any single metric. We conclude with some remarks concerning the role of multi-dimensional models in software engineering processes.

7.2   Measuring module size

7.2.1   Existing module size metrics

Structural complexity is merely one dimension, albeit an important one, of software design. As we have already remarked, it disregards component size, concentrating purely upon the manner in which components are linked. Such a view of design is potentially flawed: a designer can exploit the relationship between structure and component size by exchanging one for the other. Some notion of component size is, therefore, an important addition to a structural metric.

The preceding chapter — and also Ince and Shepperd,[90] Shepperd,[182] and Shepperd and Ince[186] — have highlighted some of the problems of only measuring architectural complexity. For example, in an empirical study of 13 different architectures that implement a single specification, we found two aberrant systems that deviated from a generally well-defined relationship between structural complexity (measured as the information flows between system components) and development effort.[182] Closer examination revealed that both architectures involved exploited a trade-off between structural complexity and component size. In one case a single module comprised 43% of the resultant software system size, measured as executable lines of code (ELOC) and was more than 600% over the mean module size. As a consequence, the structural metric underestimated development time to a significant degree. At a theoretical extreme one could minimize structural complexity by adopting an architecture containing only a single component!

The problem then becomes one of how can we measure system component size at this early stage in the software development process; and having done so, how can this measure be combined with the structure measure? The following sections attempt to provide some answers.

Several existing design metrics have attempted to combine a measure of both system structure and component size. The original information flow metric of Henry and Kafura[82, 83] attempted to do this by multiplying the information flow, or structural complexity of a module, by its size measured as estimated LOC. This gives rise to two problems. First, LOC is not available at design time. Second, empirical work has been very equivocal as to the merits of introducing the LOC term to the equation.[82, 102, 164] One can draw two possible inferences from this second problem. Either LOC is a poor measure of component size, or multiplication is an inappropriate method of combining the two dimensions of design, as they are not completely orthogonal. We are inclined to the view that both inferences contain a degree of truth.

Card and Agresti[31] have attempted to tackle the problem by defining separate metrics for inter-modular (structural) complexity and intra-modular complexity (design component size). The inter-modular measure is based on the square of the count of module calls made by each module. The intra-modular measure is the workload of a module which, from the classical module-as-a-function perspective, can be interpreted as the mapping from the set of inputs to the set of outputs. The amount of work to be performed can then be characterized as the cardinality of the two sets divided by the number of subordinate modules plus one, as this indicates the extent to which work is shared between modules. This leads to the size measure:

$$v/(f+1) \qquad (7.1)$$

where v is equal to *inputs + outputs* and f is the number of subordinate modules

Unfortunately, the metric is still vulnerable to the use of very large modules. Since workload is defined as the movement of data across the module boundary, it will fail to capture any work that is completely internal to a module. The metric also assumes that data and modules are of uniform size. Another difficulty is that for many applications, workload includes device management. Evidently, the definition of workload, or inputs and outputs, must be broadened to include devices and global data structures. Even with these changes it is disappointing to report that it performed poorly on our empirical data. The measure failed to identify two rogue modules, and produced no meaningful correlation with module size in terms of LOC, decision counts or the number of variables used. There are two possible explanations. First, increasing the number of subordinates may increase the workload of a module, as work is involved in scheduling the module calls. Second, it is vulnerable to the practice of splitting work across two or more levels of a module hierarchy; thus, a large number of subordinates might indicate a large number of partial functions to be added to the calling module's workload.

Samson *et al.*[167] describe an attempt to obtain useful measures from an OBJ specification. Unfortunately, the use of algebraic specifications is hardly a commonplace industrial activity, nor is the empirical support overwhelming. Furthermore, we have doubts concerning the validity of the underlying model which suggests that the number of axioms within the specification will be equivalent to the cyclomatic number of the code implementation.

The function point metric[2] represents another approach to specification measurement. Here the aim is to try to quantify task size using inputs such as the number of queries, system inputs, and system outputs. This measure is more flexible in the type of specification document it may be derived from, but treats a system as a single entity, whereas our interest is component and component size. By contrast, deMarco's, somewhat curiously termed, 'Bang' metric[47] can be applied at a component level, but requires a data flow diagram and entity–relationship diagrams as input. Although these notations are more widespread than formal specification notations, they still represent a minority practice; this, coupled with the fact that the authors are unaware of any empirical support for deMarco's ideas, makes the approach difficult to evaluate at present.

7.2.2   The 'work' metric

None of the previously described specification measures fully meet our requirements of relating functional requirements to modules in the design in order to give an indication of size. We have therefore developed our own approach based upon the concept of module 'work'. From any specification document it is possible to isolate the functional requirements for a proposed system. Note that functional requirements, for example that a report must be produced, are distinct from constraints such as the mean response time, as the latter typically impact most, if not all, of a system, whereas a functional requirement may be mapped on to one or a small number of components.

Functional requirements can be constructed into a hierarchy as exemplified by the Automated Requirements Traceability System developed at the Lockheed Corporation.[49] A requirement is either primitive, in that it is not refined into sub-requirements, or it is composite. For example, *Handle-Input* could be a composite requirement comprising of *Fetch-Input* and *Validate-Input*. A composite requirement is regarded as being satisfied when all its sub-requirements are satisfied, so *Handle-Input* is satisfied when both *Fetch-Input* and *Validate-Input* are satisfied. In this manner, requirements satisfaction is inherited up the hierarchy until the top level, when, by definition, all requirements are satisfied.

For each module we specify the set of primitive requirements satisfied by a module i as P_i. This set may have zero or more members, though the empty set for childless modules should be regarded with some suspicion, as this suggests either that the module has no purpose (improbable), or that a functional requirement has not been identified or allocated to that module (more probable). Another possibility is that a primitive requirement maps to more than one module, indicating either a split function or redundancy. Finally, a module may only partially satisfy a primitive requirement. In such a circumstance the primitive is treated as a composite, and new primitives are introduced. Where many primitive requirements map to many modules, this is indicative of the requirements hierarchy being insufficiently detailed. Alternatively, the design structure exhibits problems of module coupling.[195, 220] The converse is, of course, that many primitive requirements mapping to a single module is suggestive of the module hierarchy being insufficiently detailed. This is also the first intimation that the designer may have traded structural complexity for component size.

We must now consider the scheduling side of a module's workload. Scheduling work is required if one or more of three conditions are true for a module:

- two or more primitive requirements are satisfied;
- one primitive requirement is satisfied combined with one delegated requirement;
- two or more delegated requirements are combined.

A requirement is delegated if it is satisfied by a subordinate module.

We define the workload for module i, $work_i$ as:

$$work_i = r_i + \alpha(s_i) \tag{7.2}$$

$$r_i = \text{card} P_i \tag{7.3}$$

$$s_i = \text{card } Rmax_i + \text{card } Rmin_i \tag{7.4}$$

where: card is the set cardinality operator, $\alpha > 0$ is the coefficient indicating the relative contributions to workload of scheduling and requirement satisfaction; P_i is the set of primitive requirements satisfied by module i; $Rmax_i$ is the set of all requirements satisfied or inherited by the ith module; and $Rmin_i$ is the minimal set of requirements after all possible substitutions of more primitive requirements from $Rmax_i$ by higher-order or more composite requirements, for example $Rmax_i = \{a, b, c\}$ and $D = \{a, b\}$ yields $Rmin_i = \{D, c\}$.

The steps involved in calculating the work for each module may be summarized as follows (for a more detailed treatment see Shepperd[181] and Shepperd and Ince[186]):

1. Construct a functional requirements hierarchy from the system specification.
2. Construct a module calling hierarchy from the design documentation.
3. For each module determine which primitive requirements are satisfied either in full, or in part, thereby establishing P_i.
4. For each module calculate $Rmax_i$, that is, P_i plus any inherited requirements.
5. For each module calculate $Rmin_i$, that is, $Rmax_i$ with all more primitive requirement groupings replaced by higher-level requirements wherever possible. Thus: $\mathsf{card}\,Rmax_i \geq \mathsf{card}\,Rmin_i$.
6. Calculate the scheduling work of each module s_i as: $\mathsf{card}\,Rmax_i + \mathsf{card}\,Rmin_i$.
7. Calculate $work_i$ for each module as: $r_i + \alpha(s_i)$.

A judgement has to be made concerning the value of the coefficient α. This will depend largely on the type of application and development environment. As an initial approximation, and no more than that, we took the view that the ratio of work involved in scheduling in relation to carrying out a task was 1:3, and so assigned a value of 0.33 to the coefficient. This was derived as follows. First, we found that approximately 35–40% of the code appeared to be devoted to scheduling work, as opposed to satisfying primitive requirements. We also observed that the ratio of primitive tasks to scheduling tasks was, in each case, close to 1:2. This suggests that:

$$(0.375/2) : (0.625/1) \approx 1 : 3 \approx .33$$

Further empirical work is required to substantiate this approach. Indeed, it would be surprising if α does not vary for different environments and applications, since the proportion and type of scheduling work differs considerably between, say, commercial data processing systems and time-critical, embedded control systems.

7.3   Validation of the 'work' metric

So far we have a putative model for module size at design time. The next step is to assess the validity of the model. This is accomplished by a combination of theoretical techniques based upon an axiomatic statement of the desired model properties, and proofs that the axioms are satisfied. This is complemented by an empirical validation to increase our confidence that the model does indeed capture size aspects of modules identified within a software design.

7.3.1   *Theoretical validation*

So far, our model of module size has been presented in a semi-formal manner. However, in order to compare desired model characteristics with actual behaviour, using the flexible axiomatic approach outlined in the preceding chapters, a more rigorous set of definitions is required, based upon an equational rewrite system.[72] This is similar to the treatment given to the structural design metric $if4$ in the preceding chapter.

As in all algebraic specifications, the starting point is identification of the constructor operations.[68] In this instance there are two groups of constructors: those concerned with the functional requirements hierarchy derived from a specification, and those concerned with the module calling hierarchy extracted from the system architecture, or high-level design. These operations have the following signatures:

$$
\begin{aligned}
newspec: &\qquad \rightarrow spec \\
addr: req \times req \times spec &\qquad \rightarrow spec \\
newdes: &\qquad \rightarrow des \\
addm: mod \times mod \times des &\qquad \rightarrow des \\
sat: mod \times req \times des &\qquad \rightarrow des
\end{aligned}
$$

The $newspec$ and $newdes$ operations create new hierarchies and are necessary to introduce determinism into the specification. $addr$ and $addm$ add requirements and modules, respectively, to an existing hierarchy. Since a hierarchy is a structure that requires all its elements to be related, the second argument is the parent of the requirement or module being added.*

The constructor sat is important because it represents the mapping or linkage between the two hierarchies, whereby a module from the design satisfies a functional requirement from the specification. There is no reason, in principle, why one module may not satisfy zero, one or many requirements, nor why one requirement should not be implemented by one or more modules.† In the interests of brevity and clarity it is assumed that we are only dealing with well-formed structures, that is, a sub-set of all structures that it is possible to describe using the constructor operations. Specifically, it is assumed that the design fully satisfies its specification, that the hierarchies contain no recursive structures, and that all requirement and module names are unique. This avoids the need to introduce internal operations and their attendant complications, although the algebraic technique can handle such situations — as evidenced by the specification of the $if4$ metric given in the preceding chapter.

---

*This style of constructor presents one difficulty in the form of the root node, or top-level element. It is resolved by the use of a special null parent value represented by the empty string. The justification for this slight unpleasantness is that it simplifies the algebraic specification greatly by reducing the number of constructors from six to four.

†The pathological case of a design failing to satisfy its specification fully — that is, a requirement being implemented by zero modules — is excluded from the following discussion on the grounds that the model will not yield meaningful metrics in such circumstances.

The description of the model from the last section has the fundamental concept of a requirement comprising zero or more sub-requirements. This is captured by an operation that yields the set of sub-requirements that are immediately subordinate to a given requirement. Thus we have

$$comprises : req \times spec \quad \rightarrow reqset$$

where $reqset$ is a type: a set of requirements. Note, that as a form of short-hand this model specification assumes that the sets and their basic operations, such as membership, union, and subset are defined previously. Again, this is in the interests of brevity. The equations to define the $comprises$ operation are based upon the constructors operations already described:

$$
\begin{aligned}
comprises(r_1, newspec) \quad &= \quad \{\} \\
comprises(r_1, addr(r_2, r_3, S)) \quad &= \quad \text{if } r_1 = r_3 \\
&\qquad \text{then } comprises(r_1, S) \cup \{r_2\} \\
&\qquad \text{else } comprises(r_1, S)
\end{aligned}
$$

Next we define the operator $exists?$, which tests to see if a given requirement is contained within the requirements hierarchy:

$$exists?: req \times spec \quad \rightarrow boolean$$

$$
\begin{aligned}
exists?(r_1, newspec) \quad &= \quad \text{false} \\
exists?(r_1, addr(r_2, r_3, S)) \quad &= \quad \text{if } r_1 = r_2 \text{ then true} \\
&\qquad \text{else } exists?(r_1, S)
\end{aligned}
$$

It is also useful to define requirements as either primitive, that is, without sub-requirements, or as composite. An operation $prim?$ returns true if a given requirement is primitive.

$$prim?: req \times spec \quad \rightarrow boolean \cup \{\text{error}\}$$

$$
\begin{aligned}
prim?(r_1, newspec) \quad &= \quad \{\text{error}\} \\
prim?(r_1, addr(r_2, r_3, S)) \quad &= \quad \text{if } \neg exists?(r_1, S) \\
&\qquad \text{then error} \\
&\qquad \text{else} \\
&\qquad\qquad \text{if } comprises(r_1, S) = \{\} \\
&\qquad\qquad \text{then true} \\
&\qquad\qquad \text{else false}
\end{aligned}
$$

This definition merely states that for any non-empty specification structure, any requirement that has no sub-requirements is deemed to be a primitive. The operation is meaningless if the specification structure is empty, or does not contain the requirement r_1, and this is indicated by the special result $\{\text{error}\}$ which terminates the equation rewriting.

Next we turn to the module calling hierarchy and define the operation which returns the set of all modules directly called by a given module within a system architecture:

$$calls: mod \times des \quad \rightarrow modset$$

$$calls(m_1, newdes) \qquad = \qquad \{\}$$
$$calls(m_1, addm(m_2, m_3, D)) = \qquad \text{if } m_1 = m_3$$
$$\text{then } calls(m_1, D) \cup m_2$$
$$\text{else } calls(m_1, D)$$
$$calls(m_1, sat(m_2, r_1, D)) \qquad = \qquad calls(m_1, D)$$

The last equation states essentially that the operation *sat* has no effect upon the module calling structure. The specification has been slightly simplified by ignoring the possibility of a module that does not exist within a non-empty calling hierarchy. In such a circumstance an empty set would be returned. Note that this algebraic specification makes it clear that any subordinate module that is invoked more than once will only be counted as one call — since a set may not have duplicate members. However, a module may be called by more than one set, in which case it will be a member of more than *modset*.

The next operation *descend?* is related to calls, in that it tests whether module m_1 is a descendant of module m_2, where *descendant* means a calling path of arbitrary length* from the latter to the former module. An additional, internal operation is present in order to create a second copy of the argument *des* which is passed down the recursion as a consequence of the stateless style of specification. In other words, it is an internal arte-fact of the algebraic specification and is not, therefore, a direct external characteristic of the model:

$$descend?: \; mod \times mod \times des \qquad \rightarrow boolean$$
$$desc?: \; mod \times mod \times des \times des \qquad \rightarrow boolean$$

The axioms are:

$$descend?(m_1, m_2, D) \qquad = \qquad desc?(m_1, m_2, D, D)$$

$$desc?(m_1, m_2, newdes, D) \quad = \qquad \text{false}$$
$$desc?(m_1, m_2, addm(m_3, m_4, D_1), D)$$
$$= \qquad \text{if } ((m_1 = m_3) \wedge ((m2 = m4)) \vee$$
$$(desc?(m_2, m_4, D_1, D)) \wedge$$
$$(m4 \neq \prime \prime))$$
$$\text{then true}$$
$$\text{else } desc?(m_1, m_2, D_1, D)$$
$$desc?(m_1, m_2, sat(m_3, r_1, D_1), D)$$
$$= \qquad desc?(m_1, m_2, D_1, D)$$

Now we define the set of primitive requirements directly satisfied by a given module, in terms of the operation *Pwork*:

$$Pwork: \; mod \times des \times spec \qquad \rightarrow reqset$$

The axioms are:

---

*desc? is distinct from *calls* in that *calls* returns only those modules that are directly called by the specified module, that is, a calling path length of one.

$$Pwork(m_1, newdes, S) = \{\}$$
$$Pwork(m_1, D, newspec) = \{\}$$
$$Pwork(m_1, sat(m_2, r_1, D), S)$$

$$= \text{if } (m_1 = m_2)\wedge$$
$$comprises(r_1, S) = \{\}$$
$$\text{then } Pwork(m_1, D, S) \cup \{r_1\}$$
$$\text{else } Pwork(m_1, D, S)$$

$$Pwork(m_1, addm(m_2, m_3, D), S)$$
$$= Pwork(m_1, D, S)$$

The next concept from the model that requires formalizing is that of inheritance whereby a module inherits the requirement satisfactions of all its descendants, not merely those modules that it directly calls. This is captured by the operation *inherits* and the internal operation *inherit*:

$$\text{inherits: } mod \times des \quad\rightarrow reqset$$
$$\text{inherit: } mod \times des \times des \quad\rightarrow reqset$$

The axioms are:

$$inherits(m_1, D) = inherit(m_1, D, D)$$

$$inherit(m_1, newdes, D) = \{\}$$
$$inherit(m_1, addm(m_2, m_3, D_1), D)$$
$$= inherit(m_1, D_1, D)$$
$$inherit(m_1, sat(m_2, r_1, D_1), D)$$

$$= \text{if } desc?(m_2, m_1, D)$$
$$\text{then } inherit(m_1, D_1, D) \cup \{r_1\}$$
$$\text{else } inherit(m_1, D_1, D)$$

Note that this definition means that a module does not inherit the requirements that it directly satisfies, and, consequently, leaf modules — those without descendants — do not inherit.

The next step is to define the process of factoring out groups of requirements and substituting them by more abstract requirements:

$$\text{abs: } reqset \times spec \quad\rightarrow reqset$$
$$\text{abstract:} reqset \times spec \times spec \quad\rightarrow reqset$$

The axioms are:

$$abs(R, S) = abstract(R, S, S)$$

$$abstract(\{\}, S_1, S) = \{\}$$
$$abstract(R, newspec, S) = R$$
$$abstract(R, addr(r_1, r_2, S_1), S)$$

$$= \text{if } comprises(r_1, S) \neq \{\}\wedge$$
$$(comprises(r_1, S) \subseteq R)$$
$$\text{then } abstract(R, S_1, S)$$
$$\cup R \cup \{r_1\} - comprises(r_1, S)$$

else $abstract(R, S_1, S)$

Finally, we proceed to define the two outputs from the model, $work_i$ and $work$, where $work_i$ is a measure of workload or size for the mth module and $work$ is a measure for the entire system:

$$work_i\colon mod \times spec \times des \qquad\qquad \to real$$
$$work\colon spec \times des \qquad\qquad\qquad \to real$$
$$wk\colon spec \times des \times des \qquad\qquad \to real$$

The axioms are:

$$work_i(m_1, newspec, D) \quad = \quad 0$$
$$work_i(m_1, S, newdes) \quad = \quad 0$$
$$work_i(m_1, S, D) \quad = \quad \mathsf{card}\ (Pwork(m_1, D, S))$$
$$+\alpha(\mathsf{card}(\mathsf{abs}(inherits(m_1, D)$$
$$\cup Pwork(m_1, D, S), S))$$
$$+\mathsf{card}(inherits(m_1, D)$$
$$\cup Pwork(m_1, D, S)))$$

$$work(S, D) \quad = \quad wk(S, D, D)$$

$$wk(S, newdes, D) \quad = \quad 0$$
$$wk(S, addm(m_1, m_2, D_1), D) = \quad wk(S, D_1, D)$$
$$+work_i(m_1, S, D)$$
$$wk(S, sat(m_1, r_1, D_1), D) \quad = \quad wk(S, D_1, D)$$

This concludes the formal definition of the model, a full description can be found in Shepperd.[183] The next step is to consider those properties that we wish to be true of the model and state them as axioms. We will then attempt to demonstrate whether the axioms hold for the model using a similar approach to that demonstrated in the preceding chapter.

The next step is to carry out an evaluation. By applying the three tiered approach of the flexible axiomatic method described in the preceding chapter we obtain those axioms that are fundamental to all measurement as described in Chapter 4. Briefly these are:

Axiom 7.1 *It must be possible to describe, even if not formally, the rules governing the measurement.*

Axiom 7.2 *The measure must generate at least two equivalence classes so that the metric is able to discriminate between software designs.*

Axiom 7.3 *An equality relation is required.*

Axiom 7.4 *There must exist two or more designs that will be assigned to the same equivalence class.*

This is a stricter form of Axiom 7.3. If this cannot be shown to be true the metric will generate a unique value for each unique design — not a very useful property for a software metric.

Axiom 7.5 *The metric must not produce anomalies (i.e. the metric must preserve empirical orderings), so if module A can be shown to be empirically larger than module B, then this must be mirrored by the metric values for modules A and B.* This is known as the Representation Theorem.[118]*

Axiom 7.6 *The Uniqueness Theorem must hold[199] for all permissible transformations for the particular scale type — in this instance an ordinal scale.*

Next are those axioms that are dependent upon the choice of measurement scale. In this instance the relationships identified within the model are concerned with input and output variable ranks, which, in turn, suggests that weak ordering will be sufficient for our purposes. This implies ordinal measurement. The axioms are those of transitivity of the $<$ and $>$ relations and symmetry, reflexivity, and transitivity of the equivalence relation.

Lastly, there are those axioms that relate to the specific model underlying the measure in question. Again, it is possible to provide categories under which axioms may be selected. These are:

- resolution;
- empirically meaningless structures;
- model invariants.

No further axioms concerning measurement resolution are required beyond the axioms which state that the measure must be capable of discrimination and the axiom that states that there must exist at least two system architectures that will be assigned to the same equivalence class.

Concerning meaninglessness: this category of axioms will be avoided as a consequence of the decision to simplify the model by not defining illegal or meaningless structures explicitly, for example where the specification is not fully implemented by the design. Consequently, no axioms are offered.

The third category of axioms are those properties specific to this model which we believe are of fundamental significance and thus must remain invariant. To elaborate:

Axiom 7.7 *Adding an additional requirement to the system specification must increase the work metric.*

$$\forall S \in spec; D \in des; r \in req; m \in mod \bullet$$
$$satspec(D, S) \Rightarrow work(S, D) < work(addr(S), sat(m, r, D))$$

---

*The nub here is whether it is possible to show empirically that $A > B$. The major limitation to the usefulness of this axiom is the difficulty of obtaining agreement on the empirical relational system. Frequently it is not obvious that A is larger than B, and much depends upon our intuitive understanding of module size. Accuracy of measurement is another problem area. The situation is even more ambiguous for such metaphysical commodities as complexity; perhaps one should argue for a homomorphism between a metaphysical relational system and the measurement system.

This axiom requires a further operation for the algebraic definition of the model of software design size. This is required to test that a design satisfies a given specification. Note that in order to define the *satspec* operation two internal operations are required, *satspec'* and *satreq*.

$satspec: des \times spec \qquad\qquad \rightarrow boolean$

$satspec': des \times spec \times spec \qquad \rightarrow boolean$
$satreq: des \times req \qquad\qquad\quad \rightarrow boolean$

$$satreq(newdes, r_1) \qquad\qquad = \qquad\qquad false$$
$$satreq(addm(m_1, m_2, D), r_1) = \qquad\qquad satreq(D, r_1)$$
$$satreq(sat(m_1, r_2, D), r_1) \qquad = \qquad\qquad \text{if } r_1 = r_2$$
$$\text{then true}$$
$$\text{else } satreq(D, r_1)$$

$$satspec(D, S) \qquad\qquad\qquad = \qquad\qquad satspec'(D, S, S)$$

$$satspec'(D, newspec, S) \qquad = \qquad\qquad true$$
$$satspec'(newdes, addr(r_1, r_2, S_1), S)$$
$$= \qquad\qquad false$$
$$satspec'(D, addr(r1, r2, S1), S)$$
$$= \qquad\qquad \text{if } prim?(r1, S)$$
$$\text{then}$$
$$\qquad \text{if } satreq(r_1, D)$$
$$\qquad \text{then } satspec'(D, S_1, S)$$
$$\qquad \text{else false}$$
$$\text{else } satspec'(D, S_1, S)$$

Axiom 7.8 *The metric $work_i$ must increase when the ith module satisfies an additional requirement:*

$$\forall i \in mod; r_1, r_2 \in req; S \in spec; D \in des \bullet$$
$$work_i(i, S, D) < work_i(i, adds(r_1, r_2, S), sat(i, r_1, D))$$

Axiom 7.9 *There must exist different designs that satisfy the same specification, but that have different work metric values. In other words, design size is not only a function of the specification, but also the intrinsic organization of the design.*

The consequence of this axiom is that for a given specification, choice of architecture can influence size:

$$\exists D_1, D_2 \in des; S \in spec \bullet$$
$$satspec(D_1, S) \wedge satspec(D_2, S) \Rightarrow work(S, D_1) \neq work(S, D_2)$$

It is noteworthy that the model of design size has fewer axioms associated with it than the model of design structure presented in the preceding
chapter. The likely explanation is that size is a somewhat simpler concept than those of structure and flows of information coupling modules
together. Nevertheless, there remains the question of whether the axioms
listed above are sufficient. To some extent the question is unanswerable,
since the desired behaviour of the model is merely the collection of intuitions and hypotheses floating around within the head of its progenitor!
The method of metric development outlined in this book does offer some
safeguards. These are in the form of axioms that must be true of all metrics and categories for the generation of axioms specific to the model. For
example, axioms may be required for the level of resolution of the metric. Consequently, one can have a reasonable degree of confidence that the
axioms presented at least describe some minimal set of model behaviour
characteristics.

7.3.2 Consistency of model axioms

The next step is to show that the nine axioms described in the preceding
section hold for the model of design size.

Axiom 7.1 *It must be possible to describe, even if not formally, the rules
governing the measurement.*

This is satisfied by the existence of an algebraic definition of the work
metric.*

Axiom 7.2 *The measure must generate at least two equivalence classes.*

This axiom demands an existence-type proof, that is, it is only necessary
to postulate two structures that yield different metrics in order to establish
the validity of this proposition. This obligation is satisfied by the null or
empty design that has a measurement value of work equal to zero, while
a design that satisfies a single functional requirement and composed of a
single module will have a value of work approximately equal to 1.67. The
formal proof of this can be found in Shepperd.[183]

Axiom 7.3 *An equality relation is required.*

No proof is offered as the relation is axiomatic to our algebraic system,
along with propositional logic and natural numbers.

Axiom 7.4 *There must exist two or more structures that will be assigned
to the same equivalence class.*

To satisfy this, all that is required is to find two different design structures
and specifications that they fulfil which yield the same measurement. Two
such structures are shown in Figure 7.1. In this contrived example, both

---

*Furthermore, this definition has been shown to be fully operational by transforming
the algebra into statments in the language OBJ and executing the program.

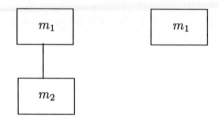

FIG. 7.1. An example of two designs that satisfy Axiom 7.4.

designs are based upon the same specification, but the first design comprises an additional module m_2 which satisfies no functional requirement. Both designs have identical work metric values and, consequently, the axiom is shown to be true because examples of different designs have been given that are members of the same equivalence class — in this case the class with a value of 1.67 — for the work metric.

Axiom 7.5 *The metric must not produce anomalies, i.e. the metric must preserve empirical orderings.*

Since the measurement system is based upon the number system of natural numbers this is satisfied.* For the proof refer to Krantz *et al.*[118]

Axiom 7.6 *The Uniqueness Theorem must hold[199] for all permissible transformations for the particular scale type.*

That is, there is a homomorphism between the transformed and the measurement structures. The underlying question is whether the measurement system is adequate for the type of measurement scale selected. For an ordinal scale the measurement structure must be order preserving for any monotonically increasing transformation function. This is trivially true.[118, 193, 199]

Axiom 7.7 *Adding an additional requirement to the system specification must increase the work metric:*

$$\forall S \in spec; D \in des; r \in req; m \in mod\bullet$$
$$satspec(D, S) \Rightarrow work(S, D) < work(addr(S), sat(m, r, D))$$

Essentially there are two parts to this proof. First, it must be shown that if specification S is implemented by design D, then adding a new

---

*In practice this axiom only becomes non-trivial when the measurement system is based upon such mathematical exotica as vectors, when it is not at all obvious that the Representation Theorem holds (for example, Hansen's modification to the cyclomatic measure[78]). This axiom assumes away the problem of errors in the measurement process; however, with the application of software measurement tools any errors will at least be systematic.

requirement to S implies adding a requirement satisfaction operation *sat* to D. The design may also be augmented by an additional module, but this is incidental to our argument, as will become apparent.* Second, it must be shown that if the number of *sat* operations for design D is increased, then the work metric must also increase for D. Since the required proof is universal in nature, induction will be employed. The base case is a null specification S and design D, while the $n + 1$ case is a requirement concatenated to S and a module to D. The full proof of this is presented in Shepperd,[183] where it is shown that the axiom holds for the base case and for the $n + 1$ case and, therefore, by inductive reasoning, for all cases.

Axiom 7.8 *The metric $work_i$ must increase when the ith module satisfies an additional requirement.*

In other words the module specification has increased:

$$\forall i \in mod; r_1, r_2 \in req; S \in spec; D \in des\bullet$$
$$work_i(i, S, D) < work_i(i, adds(r_1, r_2, S), sat(i, r_1, D))$$

Since this axiom is extremely similar to the preceding axiom the proof will be omitted. The work metric for the system is the sum of the metric values for individual modules; this can be seen in the preceding proof in that the work operation reduces to the sum of the $work_i$ operations for each *addm* operation. Thus, we have already considered the more general case and Axiom 7.8 may be seen as a specific instance of Axiom 7.7.

Axiom 7.9 *There must exist different designs that satisfy the same specification, but which have different work metric values.*

In other words, design size is not only a function of the specification, but also of the intrinsic organization of the design. The consequence of this axiom is that, for a given specification, choice of architecture can influence size:

$$\exists D_1, D_2 \in des; S \in spec\bullet$$
$$satspec(D_1, S) \land satspec(D_2, S) \Rightarrow work(S, D_1) \neq work(S, D_2)$$

Doubtless, by this stage, the reader will be grateful to note that proof of the validity of this axiom for the model is an existential one; we merely have to find two designs for which the axiom holds in order to establish its validity. In order to reduce the length of the proof further, the last example employed to establish Axiom 7.7 will be reutilized along with a different design to implement the same specification; this is shown in Figure 7.2. The specification common to both designs, S is:

$$addr(r_1, \prime\prime, addr(r, \prime\prime, newspec))$$

*It is the *sat* operation and not the *addm* operation that increases the value of $work_i$.

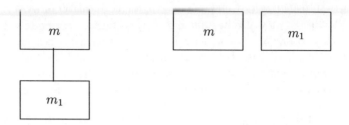

FIG. 7.2. An example of a different design that satisfies the same specification.

The first design, D_1, with a known work metric value of 3.33, is:

$$sat(m_1, r_1, addm(m_1, \prime\, \prime, sat(m, r, addm(m, \prime\, \prime, newdes)))))$$

while the second design, D_2, is formally described as:

$$sat(m_1, r_1, addm(m1, m, sat(m, r, addm(m, \prime\, \prime, newdes)))))$$

The difference between the designs lies in the fact that in the first design
D_2, module m_1 is a subordinate of module m and, as a consequence, m
inherits the requirement satisfaction of module m and therefore has to
do scheduling work, the result of which is a higher work metric value.
Consequently, Axiom 7.9 stands.

To summarize the progress from our theoretical treatment of the model:
it has been formally defined by means of an algebra, the desired properties
of the model have been given as a set of nine axioms, and then each axiom
has been demonstrated to be true by means of a reasoned proof. This
suggests that there are some grounds for confidence in the model, and that
it is appropriate to progress to an empirical evaluation. Once again it
must be emphasized, however, that a theoretical treatment is in no way
seen as a substitute for — but rather as complementary to — empirical
validation. There are two reasons why this is so. First, the proofs are
in many cases lengthy, and so the possibility that they may contain flaws
cannot be ignored. Second, the axiom set that describes the desired model
behaviour may not cover all significant model characteristics. Third, the
model may not capture all relevant factors, for example the 'work' metric
does not incorporate any notion of application area, yet this might be
highly influential in terms of capturing module size accurately at design
time. Unfortunately, since a formal system is, by definition, a closed one,
our theoretical evaluation has nothing to say concerning factors external
to the model. Hence the need for empirical evaluation.

Table 7.1 *Cross-correlations of module size measures based on rank*

	Work	ELOC	Decs	Vars
ELOC	0.927			
decs	0.895	0.963		
vars	0.694	0.692	0.679	
CA	−0.141	0.067	0.018	0.205

7.3.3 *Empirical validation*

There are two areas of the model that need to be subject to empirical investigation. First, there is the relationship between the 'work' metric and size-related factors, such as traditional measures like LOC, and also other factors such as the number of variables referenced. Second, there is the question of the extent to which the 'work' metric may be used to improve the basic model of system architecture outlined in the preceding chapter. We will postpone dealing with the second area until after techniques for combining dimensions have been discussed later in this chapter.

Since the need to be able to measure module size crudely during high-level design was prompted by the discovery of a small number of 'rogue' architectures, it is appropriate to attempt to validate the 'work' metric against this data. The data is derived from the experiment to relate the information flow based metrics of design structure to the development effort and reliability described in the preceding chapter. The reader will recall that it is based upon 13 adventure game systems that were developed by teams of three or four BSc Computer Science students. These ranged in size from 14 to 33 modules and from approximately 350 to 1000 ELOC; all were implemented in Pascal. Further details may be found in Chapter 6 and Shepperd.[182] Certain system architectures were observed to exploit the trade-off between component size and structural complexity by embedding structural complexity within components, but at the cost of having a small number of abnormally large components. Table 7.1 presents the cross-correlations between the 'work' metric and other indicators of module size where *decs* is the number of decisions, *vars* is the number of variables referenced, and *CA* is the Card and Agresti measure.[31]

We also used the upper tail of boxplots to identify abnormally large modules. Where a module was classified as abnormal for at least two out of three size indicators (ELOC, vars, and decs) the module was deemed to be a 'large' module. The 'work' metric identified eight out of nine such modules. Furthermore, only one 'non-large' module was pin-pointed incorrectly. This suggests that 'work' is a good indicator of design component size, with the caveat that it has a low resolution. In other words it is not an effective discriminator between modules of roughly equal size. This is hardly surprising given the subjective nature of tracing functional requirements to module hierarchies and the lack of homogeneity among the primitive requirements.

The above data suggests that there are good grounds for employing the 'work' metric as a crude indicator of module size at design time. The 'work' metric shows significant correlations with all three module size indicators at the 1% confidence level. In order to provide a comparison, the empirical study also investigated the Card and Agresti intra-modular metric.[31] Unlike the work metric, it reveals no significant correlations and does not appear to be a fruitful method of identifying abnormally large modules at design time.* This can be explained in part by the fact that the Card and Agresti approach ignores the effect of scheduling work upon size. Their model suggests that module size decreases as the number of subordinate modules increases. Our study found that, to the contrary, module size increases because additional code is required to control or schedule these extra subordinate modules. Clearly, without further empirical investigation — preferably industrially based — one has reservations about making extravagant claims for the work metric. Nevertheless, the model appears to have some merit, and in the absence of a better approach it will be added to the multi-dimensional model of high-level design or system architecture.

7.4   The multidimensional model

The next step is to integrate the models of module size and design structure to provide a more comprehensive picture of software design. Our intentions here are twofold. First, we intend to explore techniques for the integration of simple or uni-dimensional models and their associated metrics into more complex or multi-dimensional models. Despite increasing recognition of the need for more sophisticated approaches, for example that due to Basili and Rombach,[16] work is limited in this area. Second, we have a much more specific intention: the development of a model based upon the dimensions of size and structure to aid the software engineer at design time in the production of system architectures that are easier to implement and are more reliable.

The most typical approach to the integration of more than one model might be characterized as an abrogative method. This is based on the recognition that a single metric is an inadequate means to represent such a complex object as a software system and, consequently, the software engineer is presented with many metrics. However, the responsibility for integrating the metrics into a model is abrogated. Instead, specious analogies to car dashboards are drawn.† Essentially, the user of the metrics is being

---

*This is does not necessarily mean that the Card and Agresti approach is without merit; merely that it is unsuitable for this particular application.

†For example, Whitty has argued that the user's role is to combine, possibly disregard, and interpret the 18 metrics derived from their metrics tool QUALMS.

asked to build implicit and informal models because the researchers are unable to do so. It is arguable that this might sometimes, unfortunately, be a necessity, but it is hardly meritorious or worthy of the epithet 'science'. Examples of this method include the work of Hansen,[78] Bache and Tinker,[7] and also that of Kaposi and Myers.[105] The overwhelming problem of this type of approach lies in the task of comparison. What, for example, is one to make of the two pairs $\langle a, b \rangle$ and $\langle c, d \rangle$ where $a > c$ and $d > b$?*

The second approach might be regarded as the additive method. Again, the researchers recognize that an adequate model cannot be devised based upon a single factor but, rather, in contrast to the previous approach they attempt to combine factors additively in a numeric fashion, normally by means of weightings. This is legitimate only where factors are essentially measures of the same dimension but differ in unit.† The process of additive combination is unsound when the factors are not related to the same dimension, that is, orthogonal, because this leads to the apples and oranges type of problem where a concatenation operation cannot be defined. An example of this approach is the complexity metric of Oviedo,[150] which attempts to add control and data flow complexity.

The third approach is to map n factors on to n-dimensional space. For example, two factors can be modelled by the familiar scatter diagram. The space may then be partitioned in order to generate a classification system. The simplest method is merely to characterize values for each dimension, or factor, as outlier or non-outlier.‡ These are then combined with all other dimensions to yield a $2n$ classification scheme, where n is the number of dimensions.

This method offers two advantages. First, the model deals with the product of the dimensions, which overcomes both problems of units and orthogonality.[118] Second, it allows for a more sophisticated response by the user of the metrics. By way of illustration, one might view an abnormally large module differently, if it is also known that it has a very simple interface with the remainder of the system architecture, than if the interface were complex. In the first instance the module might be considered as a strong candidate for partitioning. In the second instance a complete redesign

---

*A further problem emerges from the absence of any well-defined relational operator, other than equality, in that the metric fails to satisfy the Uniqueness Theorem for any scale other than nominal. Consequently, this type of metric would fail to satisfy the majority of axioms outlined previously in this book.

†An example might be where length is measured in part in metres and in part in inches. The use of weightings would allow one to arrive at an integrated measure of length, in this case by multiplying inches by approximately 39. A software engineering example is the different weightings assigned to the constituent counts of Albrecht's function point metric.[2]

‡In other words, abnormal or normal. Kitchenham,[111] Kitchenham and Linkman,[115] and Linkman and Walker,[124] contain a discussion of outlier analysis techniques.

Table 7.2 *A fourfold classification of modules*

$if4_m$ value	Work value	Number
low $if4m$	low work	43 modules
low $if4m$	high work	4 modules
high $if4m$	low work	5 modules
high $if4m$	high work	10 modules

might be more appropriate. This approach has been exploited successfully by Kitchenham *et al.*[115, 114]

Using this third approach, we combined both size (*work*) and structure ($if4_m$) metrics using a two-dimensional scatter plot diagram and simply used the upper quartile of ranked values to identify outlier or abnormal modules. This gives the fourfold classification of modules shown in Table 7.2 The low $if4_m$–low work modules are not a cause for concern to the project manager. In this study the 43 modules in this class had an average error rate of 0.07 known errors per module. This contrasts with an average error rate of 0.58 for modules drawn from the other three categories. It is important to stress that a single metric would only have identified two out of the three classes of problem module.

The problem modules vary in type according to their class. The high $if4m$–high work modules manifest the most serious design faults in that they have both a high workload and a complex interface with the remainder of the system. Such metrics would be identified as outliers by either metric in isolation. The low $if4m$–high work modules are those modules that initially motivated this work, since they exhibit the trading of structural complexity for size; in other words, much of the complexity is embedded within the module. This suggests the need for further partitioning in order to generate a maintainable and reusable system architecture. The final class are those modules that do not have a high workload, yet have a complex interface with the remainder of the system. Typically these modules arise when a single function is split between several modules, or as a consequence of a lack of data structure isolation.

The final issue that this empirical analysis raises is why do system architectures potentially contain such abnormal components? The systems under study were intended as serious pieces of software, and not merely as intellectual curios. The developers were unaware that a study was being conducted and we believe it unlikely that they were consciously exploiting the size–structural complexity trade-off. Our investigation indicates that there are three contributory causes.

First, in many instances, functions are split across two levels of the module hierarchy. Thus, the higher level, or calling modules, may contain many partial functions in addition to any scheduling that they perform.

Second, all four architectures exhibit very broad hierarchies, in one case a module has 17 children. This adds greatly to the scheduling workload of the parent module.

Third, many functions are misplaced in the module hierarchy, thereby reducing the scope for procedural abstractions. A higher-level requirement cannot be satisfied until all the sub-requirements are satisfied. This is delayed until higher up the module hierarchy if one or more sub-requirements are not within the scope of a module, and therefore cannot be inherited. The scheduling workload of calling modules is increased as the module must have knowledge concerning the details of the partial satisfaction of the requirement. Where a higher-level requirement is fully satisfied, then the calling module may regard it in a more abstract vein without the need to know about the more detailed functions that make up the requirement. This is potentially a most serious design fault, as it will have a negative impact upon ease of comprehension, maintainability, and reusability of the resultant software.

7.5 Summary

Modelling is an iterative process. An initial model — often very simple — is devised. The behaviour of the model is then examined with respect to the real world. If the model stands up to this critical examination, then it can be employed, for example, in prediction. If it does not stand up to critical examination, then factors which have been omitted in its construction are re-examined and included. What we have seen in this and the preceding chapter is an example of this iterative process. The preceding chapter described a single-dimensional model for software design which was found wanting — both by means of examining its axiomatic behaviour and by means of an empirical study. This chapter has described the development and evaluation of a more sophisticated multi-dimensional model. In particular, we have addressed the problems uncovered by the application of the validation techniques encompassed within our metrics development method. The theoretical and empirical evaluation of the enhanced multi-dimensional model indicates that this new model represents an improvement upon the earlier model. It also illustrates the iterative nature of model building, and highlights the probability that there still remains scope for further improvement.

Module 'work' has been shown to be a useful metric for the identification of abnormally large design components during the design phase of the software life-cycle. Taken on its own, the 'work' metric has a relatively low resolution. It does not distinguish effectively between components of approximately the same size. On the other hand, our empirical findings suggest that it is reliable in identifying the outlier or very large system components. This is extremely valuable when combined with other measures, such as the information flow metrics of structural complexity,[90, 182, 186] as we can now construct a multi-dimensional model of a software design.

The analysis of system structures using scatterplots of two design metrics illustrates that a system architecture may contain more than one — in this case three — distinct classes of outlier module. These classes of outliers can be used as profiles to facilitate the comparison of software designs. Furthermore, the project manager may wish to adopt different remedial actions for the different classes of outlier module. Perhaps most significant, however, is the fact that no one metric could detect modules from all three outlier classes. We conclude, therefore, that multi-dimensional modelling is a technique of some significance for the software metrologist and the software engineer alike.

The empirical study is based upon relatively small-scale software systems for one particular domain, that of interactive computer games. It is not clear to what extent these results may be translated to larger systems and other application domains. For the study of larger systems, the development of an automated software tool is an imperative, as the measuring process can become extremely onerous.

Finally, to summarize, the tracing of functional software requirements to design components provides a new perspective for understanding and measuring system architecture. Metrics derived from this mapping provide reliable insights into design component size, and, when these are used in conjunction with other design metrics, such as the structure metrics of information flow, they provide valuable help for the decision making processes undertaken by the software designer.

8

SUMMARY

Synopsis

Here we review the scope of the work described within this book, and summarize its major findings. We proceed to discuss some of the weaknesses of this research and highlight the areas of potential significance which have been uncovered but which have yet to be explored.

8.1 The research

To recap: this book has been concerned with the development and, even more important, the evaluation of a set of system architecture metrics that might provide the software designer with feedback while making design decisions. This aim has, in turn, generated another aim, which has been the derivation of a method to support the development and evaluation of software metrics in general.

The book has been restricted to product metrics only, and has concentrated upon 'function-strong' as opposed to 'data-strong' systems.* Nevertheless, it is a contention of this book that many of the principles have wider application — a point that will be expanded in the following section.

The work commenced with a detailed review and critique of accomplishments to date in the area of software engineering product metrics, with particular emphasis upon three of the best-known metrics, one of which might reasonably be regarded as the classic design or system architecture metric. Out of this analysis, recurring patterns and behaviours were observed. These suggest a method that is generally applicable for the development and evaluation of software metrics and their underlying models. The method was then used to try to solve a major problem: that of developing metrics for the designers of software architecture. The technique that this book describes offers the two-pronged approach of a theoretical and an empirical evaluation of the metrics which, in turn, has suggested further enhancements to the model.

A major outcome of this book is a method that has wider implications for the development, verification, and validation of software engineering

---

*'Function-strong' and 'data-strong' is a distinction suggested by deMarco[47] in order to distinguish between those systems characterized by procedural or functional complexity and those characterized by data complexity.

metrics in general, and could clearly include both process metrics and metrics related to data architectures* — areas that have been traditionally excluded from metrics research. A second outcome of this work has been the evolution of a model to support the decision making process undertaken by a system architect that has been verified for reasonableness and has been examined empirically — including examination within an industrial context.

8.2   The outcomes

What then has the research described in this book established? First, despite the extraordinarily large number of different metrics, and the inventiveness of workers in the field, there has been little progress in terms of metrics achieving widespread acceptance. This is the direct consequence of unsatisfactory validations. Unfortunately, it is rather easier to propose metrics than to validate them. Many of the metrics in the literature remain completely unvalidated, other than by vague conjectures and appeals by their creators to our collective intuitions.[†] Plainly, this is not the result of some communal conspiracy among the computer science fraternity, but rather is due to the absence of any agreed framework for the validation of metrics, poorly articulated underlying models, a lack of definitions — most notably of what exactly it is that is being measured — questionable experimental design, and the frequent misapplication of statistics.

Careful analysis of Halstead's Software Science metrics,[75] McCabe's cyclomatic complexity measure,[133] and the Henry and Kafura's information flow metric[81, 82] has revealed a number of recurring patterns. In each case it is unclear exactly what is being measured, and terms such as 'complexity' and 'quality' predominate. Since these can hardly be regarded as operational definitions, empirical validation becomes a rather more difficult undertaking. Thus, the same metric is validated against a whole range of different quality factors by different investigators; for example,

---

*Recent research indicates that many of the ideas derived from the modelling and measurement of functionally oriented architectures are indeed relevant to data architecture.[93, 92] For example, connections between entities in the form of relationships appear to have a significant bearing upon implementation difficulties of the resultant system.

[†]A few examples include the Myers and the Hansen modification[78] to the McCabe metric.[143] Other variations on the theme include Iyengar et al.,[96] Negrini and Sami,[146] Stetter,[191] and Sinha et al.[188] all without empirical validations. Yet another example is Harrison and Magel's attempt to combine Halstead's metric with a development of McCabe's metric based on nesting level.[79] They argue that their metric is 'more intuitively satisfying'. No further validation is offered. A more recent example of a design metric is McCabe's family of design metrics,[135] again proposed without any published empirical support. One could go on, instead however, the unconvinced reader is referred back to Chapters 2 and Chapter 3.

the information flow metric has been applied to the estimation of implementation effort,[90] coding time and changes,[102] maintainability,[104, 164, 185] comprehensibility,[164] and error incidence.[112] Although, these factors are no doubt related we cannot help wondering whether slightly more focus might expedite validation. Also, it is expecting rather a lot from what are, after all, comparatively naive models that they should be able to predict such a range of software characteristics accurately in an equally diverse range of environments and applications.

Related to the problem of unclear measurement goals are poorly articulated models. Again, using information flow as an example, it is unclear what is meant by a global data structure; there are conflicting definitions of global flows in Henry[82] as compared with the formula given in the same work. An outcome of the scant regard paid to the model underlying a metric is anomalous behaviour such as the unintentional bias — of the Henry and Kafura metric — in the counting of the parameterized or local information flows against the under-counting of global flows.[90, 182]

Returning to the empirical validations of these metrics, closer inspection reveals much of the claimed support to be illusory. This is well illustrated by examining the alleged support for the information flow metric derived from an analysis of UNIX 'error' data.[82, 84] The first problem is that the authors used change data from a new release of the UNIX operating system, not error data. There are many reasons other than error correction why code may be changed between versions of a system. Second, their analysis is based upon logarithmic class intervals and, even then, Henry and Kafura still had to make the arbitrary decision of merging the three highest classes in order to transform a correlation coefficient of $rs = 0.21$ into $rs = 0.94$. Thus an important empirical evaluation of the information flow metric rests upon a mixture of arbitrary decisions and a mere six data points.

To summarize then: there are ill-defined measurement goals, underlying models that are, in the main, implicit, and questionable empirical validations of the software metrics. These problems are common to all three metrics despite the high degree of attention that they have received from the software engineering community over the past few years. Why should this be so? The research described in this book suggests two answers. The fundamental reason has been the concentration upon the minutiae of measurement, without an equal concern for the higher-level factors such as goals and methods. The second explanation, which in many ways arises out of the first, is the lowly role accorded to the measurement model. A model captures a theory concerning the measurement application, and it is this model that provides a meaning and a context for a measurement. This is true as much for software metrics as for any other area of measurement. Given this back-drop it is hardly surprising that the majority of metrics work has been *ad hoc* and poorly validated.

This, then, was the background for the research in book. Thus, the agenda became one of:

- finding a framework to describe models that underlie software metrics;
- devising more effective techniques for the evaluation of metrics;
- developing a method to guide the would-be software metrologist in the creation, selection, and validation of software metrics.

We will discuss our findings in each area in turn.

First, we examine the framework for describing a model. As has already been noted, the vast majority of measurement models are entirely implicit. Even when some attempt has been made to present the model behind the metric these are usually incomplete in one or more respects. This research has suggested that models may be described informally under seven headings, namely:

- inputs;
- outputs;
- parameters;
- relationships;
- mappings from and on to the 'real world';
- model limitations;
- model reliability.

Almost certainly, the last three headings are the most widely ignored, yet they are all vital if the model is to have any real software engineering application, and also to enable meaningful evaluation. This book has shown how this relatively informal approach may be refined further, and the behaviour of the model formally defined in terms of inputs, outputs, parameters, and relationships between these model components. This can be accomplished by the algebraic approach of Guttag[72] and Liskov,[125] where the model is defined as an equational rewrite system, each equation representing an axiom or property of the model. Such formality would seem to be indispensable if a model is to be scrutinized adequately. The precision that it offers would also seem to be valuable for anyone proposing to build software tools to automate the measurement process. Algebraic specifications offer another advantage, in addition to precision, which is that they can easily be animated using executable specification languages such as OBJ.*

---

*The $if4$ metrics and their underlying model have been implemented by the author, using the OBJ EX environment, thereby allowing 'what if' style investigation of the model. The main disadvantage of such implementations is that they require the user to be familiar with equational rewriting and are consequently not very user-friendly. Nevertheless, they are potentially useful given the very small amount of effort required to transform the style of notation used in this book into OBJ.

The second item on the research agenda was that of metric evaluation. As the book title implies, it has been argued that this lies at the heart of the research. There is little point in defining measurement models, however formally, if there is no prospect of being able to evaluate (and, if appropriate, refine) them. Given the relatively new state of the subject area of software engineering, it would not be surprising if our model building were a highly iterative process of postulating, evaluation, and refinement. Consequently, it would seem entirely appropriate that we consider the tools and mechanisms at our disposal to carry out this evaluation. This book has tried to make three contributions in this direction.

First, evaluation is greatly facilitated if the metric is defined carefully, if it is clear what is being measured, if any model limitations or assumptions are made explicit, and if some indication is given of the required level accuracy.

Next, we have proposed an entirely novel approach to the problem of validation of the theory or model behind a metric. This we term *theoretical metric evaluation*, which makes use of algebraic model specifications. A flexible framework has been described which enables those carrying out the evaluation to evolve a set of model invariants, or properties, of the model that they wish always to be true. An example of such an invariant would be that a metric, for example size, should always increase if a further module is added to an arbitrary system architecture. It is then possible, as this book has demonstrated, to prove that the invariant holds, or that in certain circumstances it is violated. It is then up to the validators to determine whether they wish to relax the invariant or modify the model. This method has been used successfully to reveal a number of problems with the uni-dimensional model of system architecture described within this book.

One benefit of the use of axiomatic descriptions together with associated proof methods, is an extremely pragmatic one: that is, they are normally far quicker, and therefore cheaper, to conduct than industrial-scale empirical validations. For this reason alone it is suggested that they be considered prior to empirical analysis, so that if model refinements are found to be necessary these may be carried out prior to the potentially more costly empirical work. Another benefit is that it is possible to reason about all possible measurement objects, whereas empirical analyses tend to adopt a sampling approach, where, hopefully, the sample is representative of the larger population. This means that the theoretical approach might uncover a problem with a rare, but pathological, object which an empirical approach might not detect. We argue that this theoretical validation technique offers several distinct advantages over more conventional methods of model evaluation. We do not argue that it should supplant empirical validation, but, rather, that it should be regarded as complementary.

The usual approach to the problem of evaluating a measurement model is empirical. Clearly, this is an equally important method of model evaluation as is the theoretical approach, but it is one that is likely to uncover different types of problems. A weakness with formal systems is that they must, necessarily, describe closed systems. *However, it is often precisely the part of a system that is excluded from a model that can cause most modelling difficulties.* Thus, formal approaches are not effective in detecting what might be thought of as 'sins of omission'. Fortunately, it is precisely these types of problems that *an empirical analysis can successfully uncover.* This book has made no special contribution in this area, other than to suggest the characteristics whereby an empirical analysis may be judged. These are:

- the hypothesis under investigation;
- the artificiality of the data used;
- the validity of the statistics employed.

In a world of finite resources and complex interacting systems and processes the ideal cannot be attained, but at least it enables workers to decide how much importance to attach to a particular empirical result. Even in the less than ideal world that we inhabit, one would still expect an empirical validation to be capable of refuting its hypothesis and employing meaningful statistics.

The third item on the research agenda was the evolution of a method, which builds upon the pioneering work of Basili and Rombach's GQM method,[165, 16] to guide workers attempting to develop and evaluate software metrics. However, the method suggested within this book emphasizes the need to make the underlying model explicit, to evaluate, and to refine. The method comprises six stages:

- problem identification;
- construction of an informal model;
- transformation into a formal model;
- derivation of the model axioms;
- theoretical model evaluation;
- empirical model evaluation.

We have also emphasized the iterative nature of the method and, therefore, the likelihood of backtracking.

In order to consider the validity of this method, it has been applied to the problem of developing design metrics for a system architect. Two models have been proposed. A simple model based upon the $if4$ metric[182] was found to be wanting in a number of respects, and a more complex model was evolved, based upon combining two metrics: the multi-dimensional model.[186] The latter was found to satisfy all its axioms of desired model behaviour (i.e. its invariants). Furthermore, two separate empirical investigations (described earlier in the book) have shown that the metrics yield

useful engineering approximations. In relating the model to development
effort and maintenance problems, statistically significant relationships have
been found. Consequently, it has been argued that the design metrics of $if4$
and 'work', coupled with their supporting model, have utility in supporting the engineering of system architectures. Practical applications include
selecting architectures that will require less development effort, identifying
potential maintenance problem areas prior to implementation, using the
model to guide and focus restructuring and re-engineering activities for
'geriatric' software systems,* and to provide a suggested order of priority
for modules undergoing design inspection or review.[†]

In conclusion, this book has described three areas of progress. First,
a new framework for describing measurement models has been proposed.
Second, a new technique for model evaluation has been devised, based
upon the application of algebras and term rewriting. Finally, a method
has been given to guide future metrics workers through the problematic
tasks of metric development and its frequently overlooked evaluation. Not
only have these ideas been proposed, but they have also been tested on
the non-trivial task of developing system architecture metrics to guide the
designer in the task of selecting structures that are easy to develop and
maintain.

8.3   Further work

Although it has been argued that this research has made a contribution in
the software metrics arena, there are clearly weaknesses and avenues that
have yet to be explored.

Two weaknesses need to be brought to light. One is that the model-
based metric development method is relatively untested, so its worth for
other types of measurement application has yet to be demonstrated. What
this research has revealed, and what is incontrovertible, is that there is a
pressing need for methods to guide the developers and users of software
metrics. Doubtless, the methods outlined in this book can, and hopefully
will in due course, be modified, adapted, and improved upon. What is
important is to appreciate the need for method.

---

*For example, the costs of completely restructuring a system that is causing main-
tenance difficulties may be prohibitive, but the use of the $if4$ and 'work' metrics can
suggest those parts of an architecture from which most restructuring benefit would be
obtained. This capitalizes upon the idea that much of the benefit may frequently be
obtained from a small proportion of the work.

[†]If a fixed time has been allocated for a design inspection, then it is appropriate to
concentrate upon the potentially most critical components first. One of the authors has
sat in a number of inspection meetings where the ordering of the review has been driven
by execution order, from working left to right and top to bottom of a module hierarchy
chart or, even, on one occasion, in alphabetical order!

The second weakness concerns the model of system architecture evolved during the course of this research. Adherence to the model-based development method has lead to one cycle of revision. However, it may be that other empirical evaluations (particularly evaluations that conform more closely to our desiderata for empirical studies) might highlight other difficulties that call for further refinements. Again, though this is likely to be the case, it has been argued that the model developed has been the subject of methodical evaluation, and that there is at least some basis for confidence in its utility. It is not the contention of this book that the model is in some sense a definitive model of system architecture. Other work, such as Basili and Rombach[16] and Shepperd and Ince[187] suggest that there are no definitive metrics or models, but, rather, a whole multiplicity of metrics, each suited to different measurement goals and applications.

Avenues that have remained unexplored include the design of data architectures. Plainly, this is an issue of some importance given the large number of database systems in existence, and some of our early work in this area seems highly promising.[71] More significant is the lack of concern with the application of metrics and models once they have been evaluated satisfactorily. In other words, metrics researchers must also consider the issue of how these metrics are to be used by software engineers. One reason why this may become important is that by focusing solely upon a product, say a system architecture, one loses sight of the fact that the same product may enter into a number of different processes and thus take on a number of different meanings. For example, an engineer may be designing an architecture from scratch, doing some maintenance work, optimizing the architecture to enhance performance, searching for reusable components or restructuring an ageing software system. In each case, the architecture takes on a different meaning — a point not captured by our product-oriented view of measurement and modelling. Again, it may be more fruitful to look for a general framework, rather than focus too strongly upon individual metrics and applications. A possibility might be to apply some of the concepts and formalisms from the area of software engineering research known as process modelling.* The outcome might be quantitative process models that describe more precisely how metrics are to be integrated into software engineering projects.[155]

*Humphrey gives a good review[85] of this area.

APPENDIX

types

$graph$

$nodetype = (module, globalds)$

$name = string$

vars

$S_1, S_2 : graph$

$t_1, t_2 : nodetype$

$n_1, n_2, n_3, n_4 : name$

external operations

$an : graph \times nodetype \times name$	$\rightarrow graph \cup \{error\}$
$ae : graph \times name \times name$	$\rightarrow graph \cup \{error\}$
$if4 : graph$	$\rightarrow nat$
$if4_m : graph \times name$	$\rightarrow nat \cup \{error\}$
$nfl : graph$	$\rightarrow nat$
$nds : graph$	$\rightarrow nat$
$nmods : graph$	$\rightarrow nat$

internal operations

$cn : graph \times nodetype \times name$	$\rightarrow graph$
$ce : graph \times name \times name$	$\rightarrow graph$
$new :$	$\rightarrow graph$
$exists : graph \times name$	$\rightarrow boolean$
$linked : graph \times name \times name$	$\rightarrow boolean$
$isamod : graph \times name$	$\rightarrow boolean$
$isads : graph \times name$	$\rightarrow boolean$
$if4int : graph \times graph$	$\rightarrow nat$
$faninl : graph \times name$	$\rightarrow nat$
$fanoutl : graph \times name$	$\rightarrow nat$
$faning : graph \times graph \times name$	$\rightarrow nat$
$fanoutg : graph \times graph \times name$	$\rightarrow nat$
$ctglobalsin : graph \times graph \times name \times name$	$\rightarrow nat$
$ctglobalsout : graph \times graph \times name \times name$	$\rightarrow nat$

semantics

1    $an(S_1, t_1, n_1)$ $= \text{ if } exists(S_1, n_1)$

                                          $\text{then}\{error\}$

$$\text{else } cn(S_1, t_1, n_1)$$

2    $ae(S_1, n_1, n_2)$
$$= \text{ if } exists(S_1, n_1) \land$$
$$exists(S_1, n_2) \land$$
$$\neg linked(S_1, n_1, n_2) \land$$
$$n_1 \neq n_2 \land$$
$$(isamod(S_1, n_1)$$
$$\lor isamod(S_1, n_2))$$
$$\text{then } ce(S_1, t_1, n_1)$$
$$\text{else}\{error\}$$

3    $exists(new, n_1)$ $= \text{ false}$

4    $exists(cn(S_1, t_1, n_2), n_1)$
$$= \text{ if } n_1 = n_2$$
$$\text{then true}$$
$$\text{else } exists(S_1, n_1)$$

5    $exists(ce(S_1, n_2, n_3), n_1)$
$$= \text{ if } n_1 = n_2 \lor n_1 = n_3$$
$$\text{then true}$$
$$\text{else } exists(S_1, n_1)$$

6    $linked(new, n_1, n_2)$ $= \text{ false}$

7    $linked(ce(S_1, n_3, n_4), n_1, n_2)$
$$= \text{ if } n_3 = n_1 \land n_4 = n_2$$
$$\text{then true}$$
$$\text{else } linked(S_1, n_1, n_2)$$

8    $linked(cn(S_1, t_1, n_3), n_1, n_2)$ $= linked(S_1, n_1, n_2)$

9    $isamod(new, n_1)$ $= \text{ false}$

10    $isamod(cn(S_1, t_1, n_2), n_1)$
$$= \text{ if } n_1 = n_2 \land t_1 = module$$
$$\text{then true}$$
$$\text{else } isamod(S_1, n_1)$$

11    $isamod(ce(S_1, n_2, n_3), n_1)$ $= isamod(S_1, n_1)$

12    $isads(new, n_1)$ $= \text{ false}$

13    $isads(cn(S_1, t_1, n_2), n_1)$
$$= \text{ if } n_1 = n_1 \land t_1 = globalds$$
$$\text{then true}$$
$$\text{else } isads(S_1, n_1)$$

14    $isads(ce(S_1, n_2, n_3), n_1)$ $= isads(S_1, n_1)$

15    $if4(S_1)$ $= if4int(S_1, S_1)$

16    $if4int(S_1, new)$ $= 0$

17    $if4int(S_1, cn(S_2, t_1, n_1))$
$$= \text{ if } t_1 = module$$
$$\text{then } if4_m(S_1, n_1) + if4int(S_1, S_2)$$
$$\text{else } if4(S_1, S_2)$$

18    $if4int(S_1, ce(S_2, n_1, n_2))$ $= if4(S_1, S_2)$

19    $if4_m(S_1, n_1)$

$\begin{aligned} = \; & \text{if } isamod(S_1, n_1) \\ & \text{then } sqr((faninl(S_1, n_1) + faning(S_1, S_1, n_1)) \\ & *((fanoul(S_1, n_1) + fanoutg(S_1, S_1, n_1))) \\ & \text{else}\{error\} \end{aligned}$

20    $faninl(new, n_1)$ $= \; 0$

21    $faninl(ce(S_1, n_2, n_3), n_1)$

$\begin{aligned} = \; & \text{if } n_3 = n_1 \wedge isamod(n_2) \\ & \text{then } 1 + faninl(S_1, n_1) \\ & \text{else } faninl(S_1, n_1) \end{aligned}$

22    $faninl(cn(S_1, t_1, n_2), n_1)$

$= \; faninl(S_1, n_1)$

23    $fanoutl(new, n_1)$ $= \; 0$

24    $fanoutl(ce(S_1, n_2, n_3), n_1)$

$\begin{aligned} = \; & \text{if } n_2 = n_1 \wedge isamod(n_3) \\ & \text{then } 1 + fanoutl(S_1, n_1) \\ & \text{else } fanoutl(S_1, n_1) \end{aligned}$

25    $fanoutl(cn(S_1, t_1, n_2), n_1)$

$= \; fanout(S_1, n_1)$

26    $faning(S_1, new, n_1)$ $= \; 0$

27    $faning(S_1, concate(S_2, n_2, n_3), n_1)$

$\begin{aligned} = \; & \text{if } n_3 = n_1 \wedge isads(n_2) \\ & \text{then } ctglobalsin(S_1, S_2, n_1, n_2) + faning(S_1, S_2, n_1) \\ & \text{else } faning(S_1, S_2, n_1) \end{aligned}$

28    $faning(S_1, concatn(S_2, t_1, n_2), n_1)$

$= \; faning(S_1, S_2, n_1)$

29    $fanoutg(S_1, new, n_1)$ $= \; 0$

30    $fanoutg(S_1, concate(S_2, n_2, n_3), n_1)$

$\begin{aligned} = \; & \text{if } n_3 = n_1 \wedge isads(n_2) \\ & \text{then} \\ & ctglobalsout(S_1, S_2, n_1, n_2) + fanoutg(S_1, S_2, n_1) \\ & \text{else } fanoutg(S_1, S_2, n_1) \end{aligned}$

31    $fanoutg(S_1, concatn(S_2, t_1, n_2), n_1)$

$= \; fanoutg(S_1, S_2, n_1)$

32    $ctglobalsin(S_1, new, n_1, n_2)$ $= \; 0$

33    $ctglobalsin(S_1, ce(S_2, n_3, n_4), n_1, n_2)$

$\begin{aligned} = \; & \text{if } n_4 = n_2 \wedge isamod(n_3) \wedge n_3 \neq n_1 \\ & \text{then } 1 + ctglobalsin(S_1, S_2, n_1, n_2) \\ & \text{else } ctglobalsin(S_1, S_2, n_1, n_2) \end{aligned}$

34   $ctglobalsin(S_1, cn(S_2, t_1, n_3), n_1, n_2)$
$$= ctglobalsin(S_1, S_2, n_1, n_2)$$

35   $ctglobalsout(S_1, new, n_1, n_2)$ $=$ 0
36   $ctglobalsout(S_1, ce(S_2, n_3, n_4), n_1, n_2)$
$$= \text{if } n_3 = n_2 \wedge isamod(n_4) \wedge n_4 \neq n_1$$
$$\text{then } 1 + ctglobalsout(S_1, S_2, n_1, n_2)$$
$$\text{else } ctglobalsout(S_1, S_2, n_1, n_2)$$
37   $ctglobalsout(S_1, cn(S_2, t_1, n_3), n_1, n_2)$
$$= ctglobalsout(S_1, S_2, n_1, n_2)$$

38   $nds(new)$ $=$ 0
39   $nds(cn(S_1, t_1, n_1))$ $=$ if $t_1 = globalds$
$$\text{then } 1 + nds(S_1)$$
$$\text{else } nds(S_1)$$
40   $nds(ce(S_1, n_1, n_2))$ $=$ $nds(S_1)$

41   $nmods(new)$ $=$ 0
42   $nmods(cn(S_1, t_1, n_1))$ $=$ if $t_1 = module$
$$\text{then } 1 + nmods(S_1)$$
$$\text{else } nmods(S_1)$$
43   $nmods(ce(S_1, n_1, n_2))$ $=$ $nmods(S_1)$

44   $nfl(new)$ $=$ 0
45   $nfl(ce(S_1, n_1, n_2))$ $=$ $1 + nfl(S_1)$
46   $nfl(cn(S_1, t_1, n_1))$ $=$ $nfl(S_1)$

REFERENCES

1. E W Adams. On the nature and purpose of measurement. *Synthese*, 16:125–169, 1966.
2. A J Albrecht and J R Gaffney. Software function, source lines of code, and development effort prediction: a Software Science validation. *IEEE Transactions on Software Engineering*, 9(6):639–648, 1983.
3. A J Albrecht and J R Gaffney. AD/M productivity measurement and estimate validation. Report, IBM Corporate Information Systems and Administration, 1984.
4. C Alexander. *Notes on the Synthesis of Form*. Harvard University Press, 1964.
5. L J Arthur. *Measuring Programmer Productivity and Software Quality*. Wiley–Interscience, 1985.
6. C Ashworth and M Goodland. *SSADM, a Practical Approach*. McGraw-Hill, 1990.
7. R Bache and R Tinker. A rigorous approach to metrication: a field trial using KINDRA. In *Proceedings IEE/BCS Conference, Software Engineering 88*, pages 28–32, 1988.
8. C Bailey and W Dingee. A software study using Halstead metrics. *SIGMETRICS Performance Evaluation Review*, 10(1):189– 197, 1981.
9. A L Baker and S H Zweben. A comparison of measures of control flow complexity. *IEEE Transactions on Software Engineering*, 6(6):506–511, 1980.
10. N Balut, R Bayer, and M H Halstead. Experimental validation of a structural property of FORTRAN programs. In *Proceedings ACM National Conference*, pages 207–211, 1974.
11. V R Basili and D H Hutchens. An empirical study of a syntactic complexity family. *IEEE Transactions on Software Engineering*, 9(6):664–672, 1983.
12. V R Basili and B T Perricone. Software errors and complexity: an empirical investigation. *Communications of the ACM*, 27(1):42–52, 1984.
13. V R Basili and T Phillips. Evaluating and comparing the software metrics in the Software Engineering Laboratory. *SIGMETRICS Performance Evaluation Review*, 10(1):95– 106, 1981.
14. V R Basili and R W Reiter. Evaluating automatable measures of software development. In *Proceedings IEEE Workshop on Quantitative Software Models*, pages 107–116, 1979.

15. V R Basili and H D Rombach. Tailoring the software process to project goals and environments. In *Proceedings 9th International Conference on Software Engineering*, pages 345–357, 1987.

16. V R Basili and H D Rombach. The TAME project: towards improvement-oriented software environments. *IEEE Transactions on Software Engineering*, 14(6):758–773, 1988.

17. V R Basili, R W Selby, and T Phillips. Metric analysis and data validation across FORTRAN projects. *IEEE Transactions on Software Engineering*, 9(6):652–663, 1983.

18. J Beane, N Giddings, and J Silverman. Quantifying software designs. In *Proceedings 7th International Software Engineering Conference*, pages 314–322, 1984.

19. C A Behrens. Measuring the productivity of computer systems development activities with function points. *IEEE Transactions on Software Engineering*, 9(6):649–658, 1983.

20. L A Belady. On software complexity. In *Proceedings IEEE Workshop on Quantitative Models for Software Reliability, Complexity and Cost*, pages 90–94, 1979.

21. L A Belady and C J Evangelisti. System partitioning and its measure. *Journal of Systems and Software*, 1(2):23–29, 1981.

22. G Benyon-Tinker. Complexity models in an evolving large system. In *Proceedings ACM Workshop on Quantitative Models*, pages 117–127, 1979.

23. N Beser. Foundations and experiments in software science. *SIGMETRICS Performance Evaluation Review*, 11(3):48–72, 1982.

24. B Boehm. *Software Engineering Economics*. Prentice-Hall, 1981.

25. G Booch. Object-oriented design. *IEEE Transactions on Software Engineering*, 12(2):211–221, 1986.

26. G Booch. *Object-oriented Design with Applications*. Benjamin Cummings, 1991.

27. J B Bowen. Are current approaches sufficient for measuring software quality. In *Proceedings SIGMETRICS-SIGSOFT Quality Assurance Workshop*, 1978.

28. A J Bowles. Effects of Design Complexity on Software Maintenance. PhD thesis, Carnegie-Mellon University, 1983.

29. J R Brown and K F Fischer. A graph theoretic approach to the verification of program structures. In *Proceedings 3rd International Conference on Software Engineering*, pages 136–141, 1978.

30. D N Card and W W Agresti. Resolving the Software Science anomaly. *Journal of Systems and Software*, 7:29–35, 1987.

31. D N Card and W W Agresti. Measuring software design complexity. *Journal of Systems and Software*, 8:185–197, 1988.

32. D N Card, V E Church, and W W Agresti. An empirical study of software design practices. *IEEE Transactions on Software Engineering*,

12:264–271, 1986.

33. CCTA. *Estimating with MkII Function Point Analysis*, 1991.

34. N Chapin. A measure of software complexity. In *Proceedings NCC 79*, pages 995–1002, 1979.

35. E T Chen. Programmer complexity and programmer productivity. *IEEE Transactions on Software Engineering*, 4(3):187–194, 1978.

36. S R Chidamber and K F Kemerer. Towards a metrics suite for object-oriented design. In *Proceedings OOPSLA 91*, 1992.

37. K Christenson, G P Fitsos, and C Smith. A perspective on Software Science. *IBM Systems Journal*, 20(4):372–387, 1981.

38. D Comer and M H Halstead. A simple experiment in top–down design. *IEEE Transactions on Software Engineering*, 5(5):105–109, 1979.

39. S D Conte, H E Dunsmore, and V Y Shen. *Software Engineering Metrics and Models*. Benjamin Cummings, 1986.

40. N S Coulter. Software Science and cognitive psychology. *IEEE Transactions on Software Engineering*, 9(2):166–171, 1983.

41. B Curtis. In search of software complexity. In *Proceedings of the Workshop on Quantitative Software Complexity Models*, pages 95–106, 1979.

42. B Curtis, S Sheppard, P Milliman, M Borst, and T Love. Measuring the psychological complexity of software maintenance tasks with the Halstead and McCabe metrics. *IEEE Transactions on Software Engineering*, 5(2):96–104, 1979.

43. B Curtis, S Sheppard, and P Milliman. Third time charm: stronger prediction of programmer performance by software complexity metrics. In *Proceedings of the 4th International Conference on Software Engineering*, pages 356–360, 1979.

44. O J Dahl, E W Dijkstra, and C A R Hoare. *Structured Programming*. Academic Press, 1972.

45. J S Davis and R J LeBlanc. A study of the applicability of complexity measures. *IEEE Transactions on Software Engineering*, 14(9):1366–1372, 1988.

46. T deMarco. *Structured Analysis and System Specification*. Yourdon Press, 1978.

47. T deMarco. *Controlling Software Projects. Management, Measurement and Estimation*. Yourdon Press, 1982.

48. E W Dijkstra. Goto statement considered harmful. *Communications of the ACM*, 18(8):453–457, 1968.

49. M Dorfman and R F Flynn. ARTS — an automated requirements traceability system. *Journal of Systems and Software*, 4(4):63–74, 1984.

50. H E Dunsmore and J D Gannon. Experimental investigation of programming complexity. In *Proceedings 16th Annual Technical Sympo-*

sium on System Software, pages 117–125, 1977.

51. H E Dunsmore and J D Gannon. An analysis of the effects of programming factors on programming effort. *Journal of Systems and Software*, 1(2):141–153, 1979.

52. L O Ejiogu. Lemcomm softgram, a simple measure of software complexity. *SIGPLAN Notices*, 20(3), 1985.

53. J L Elshoff. Measuring commercial programs using Halstead's criteria. *SIGPLAN Notices*, 11(5):38–46, 1976.

54. T J Emerson. A discriminant metric for module cohesion. In *Proceedings 7th International Conference on Software Engineering*, pages 294–303, 1984.

55. W M Evangelist. Software complexity metric sensitivity to program structuring rules. *Journal of Systems and Software*, 3(3):231–243, 1983.

56. W M Evangelist. Program complexity and programming style. In *Proceedings IEEE Conference on Data Engineering*, pages 534–541, 1984.

57. N E Fenton. *Software Metrics: A Rigorous Approach*. Chapman and Hall, 1991.

58. N E Fenton. When is a measure not a measure. *Software Engineering Journal*, 7(5):357–362, 1992.

59. N E Fenton and A A Kaposi. An engineering theory of structure and measurement. In *Proceedings Annual Conference of the Centre for Software Reliability*, 1987.

60. N E Fenton and A A Kaposi. Metrics and software structure. *Information and Software Technology*, 29(6):301–320, 1987.

61. N E Fenton and R W Whitty. Axiomatic approach to software metrication. *Computer Journal*, 29(4):330–340, 1986.

62. N E Fenton, R W Whitty, and A A Kaposi. A generalised mathematical theory of structured programming. *Theoretical Computer Science*, 36:145–171, 1985.

63. L Finkelstein and M S Leaning. A review of the fundamental concepts of measurement. *Measurement*, 2(1):25–34, 1984.

64. A Fitzsimmons. Relating the presence of software errors to the theory of Software Science. In *Proceedings 11th Hawaii International Conference on Systems Science*, pages 40–46, 1978.

65. A Fitzsimmons. A review and evaluation of Software Science. *ACM Computing Surveys*, 10:3–18, 1978.

66. Y Funayami and M H Halstead. A Software Physics analysis of Akiyama's debugging data. In *Proceedings of the Symposium on Computer Software Engineering*, pages 133–138, 1976.

67. J E Gaffney. Program control, complexity and productivity. In *Proceedings of the Workshop on Quantitative Models for Reliability*, pages 140–142, 1979.

68. N H Gehani. Specifications: formal and informal — a case study. *Software Practice and Experience*, 12:433–444, 1982.

69. R D Gordon. Measuring improvements in program clarity. *IEEE Transactions on Software Engineering*, 5(2):79–90, 1979.

70. R D Gordon and M H Halstead. An experiment comparing FORTRAN programming times with the software physics hypothesis. In *Proceedings AFIPS Annual Conference*, pages 935–937, 1976.

71. R H M Gray, B Carey, N McGlynn, and A Pengelly. Design metrics for database systems. *British Telecom Technology Journal*, 9(4):69–79, 1991.

72. J V Guttag. Abstract data types and the development of data structures. *Communications of the ACM*, 20(6):397–404, 1977.

73. N R Hall and S Preiser. Combined network complexity measures. *IBM Journal of Research and Development*, 23(1):15–27, 1984.

74. M H Halstead. Natural laws controlling algorithmic structure. *SIGPLAN Notices*, 7(2):19–26, 1972.

75. M H Halstead. *Elements of Software Science*. Elsevier - North Holland, 1977.

76. M H Halstead. Guest editorial on Software Science. *IEEE Transactions on Software Engineering*, 5(2):74–75, 1979.

77. P G Hamer and G D Frewin. M. H. Halstead's Software Science — a critical evaluation. In *Proceedings 6th International Conference on Software Engineering*, pages 197–206, 1982.

78. W J Hansen. Measurement of program complexity by the pair (cyclomatic complexity, operator count). *SIGPLAN Notices*, 13(3):29–33, 1978.

79. W Harrison and K Magel. A complexity measure based on nesting level. *SIGPLAN Notices*, 16(3):63–74, 1981.

80. S Hartman. A counting tool for RPG. *SIGMETRICS Performance Evaluation Review*, 11:86–100, Fall 1982.

81. S Henry. Information Flow Metrics for the Evaluation of Operating Systems. PhD thesis, Iowa State University, 1979.

82. S Henry. Software metrics based on information flow. *IEEE Transactions on Software Engineering*, 7(5):510–518, 1981.

83. S Henry and D Kafura. The evaluation of systems' structure using quantitative metrics. *Software Practice and Experience*, 14(6):561–573, 1984.

84. S Henry, D Kafura, and K Harris. On the relationship among three software metrics. *SIGMETRICS Performance Evaluation Review*, 10:81–88, Spring 1981.

85. W S Humphrey. *Managing the Software Process*. Addison-Wesley, 1989.

86. R A Humphreys. Control flow as a measure of program complexity. *SCR Newsletter*, 1986.

87. D H Hutchens and V R Basili. System structure analysis; clustering with data bindings. *IEEE Transactions on Software Engineering*, 11(8):749–757, 1985.

88. D C Ince. Module interconnection languages and PROLOG. *SIGPLAN Notices*, 19(8):88–93, 1984.

89. D C Ince and M J Shepperd. System design metrics: a review and perspective. In *Proceedings Software Engineering 88*, pages 23–27, 1988.

90. D C Ince and M J Shepperd. An empirical and theoretical analysis of an information flow based design metric. In *Proceedings European Software Engineering Conference*, 1989.

91. D C Ince and M J Shepperd. Quality control of software designs using cluster analysis. In *Proceedings EOQC/SQA Conference, Management of Quality: Key to the Nineties*, 1989.

92. D C Ince and M J Shepperd. The measurement of data design. Technical report, School of Computing and IT, Wolverhampton Polytechnic, 1990.

93. D C Ince and M J Shepperd. Metricating data-oriented notations. Technical report, Computing Department, Open University, 1990.

94. D C Ince and M J Shepperd. The use of cluster techniques and system design metrics in software maintenance. In *Proceedings IT90 Conference*, 1990.

95. International Function Point Users Group. *Function Point Counting Practices Manual*, 1992.

96. S S Iyengar, J Fuller, and N Parameswaran. A measure of logical complexity of programs. *Computer Languages*, 7:147–160, 1982.

97. M A Jackson. *Principles of Program Design*. Academic Press, 1975.

98. M A Jackson. *System Development*. Prentice-Hall, 1982.

99. D B Johnston and A M Lister. A note on the Software Science length equation. *Software Practice and Experience*, 11(8), 1981.

100. C Jones. A short history of function points and feature points. Technical report, Software Productivity Research Inc., 1987.

101. C B Jones. *Systematic Software Development with VDM*. Prentice-Hall, 1986.

102. D Kafura and J T Canning. A validation of software metrics using many metrics and two resources. In *Proceedings 8th International Conference on Software Engineering*, pages 378–385, 1985.

103. D Kafura and S Henry. Software quality metrics based on interconnectivity. *Journal of Systems and Software*, 2:121–131, 1981.

104. D Kafura and G R Reddy. The use of software complexity metrics in software maintenance. *IEEE Transactions on Software Engineering*, 13(3):335–343, 1987.

105. A A Kaposi and M Myers. Quality assurance specification and design. *Software Engineering Journal*, 5(1):11–26, 1990.

106. J K Kearney, R L Sedlemeyer, R Thompson, M Gray, and A Adler. Software complexity measurement. *Communications of the ACM*, 29(11):1044–1050, 1986.

107. C F Kemerer. An empirical validation of software cost estimation models. *Communications of the ACM*, 30(5):416–429, 1987.

108. B Kernighan and P J Plauger. *The Elements of Programming Style*. McGraw-Hill, 1978.

109. B A Kitchenham. Measures of programming complexity. *ICL Technical Journal*, pages 298–316, May 1981.

110. B A Kitchenham. Towards a constructive quality model. Part I: software quality modelling, measurement and prediction. *Software Engineering Journal*, 2(4):105–113, 1987.

111. B A Kitchenham. Towards a constructive quality model. Part II: statistical techniques for modelling software quality in the ESPRIT REQUEST project. *Software Engineering Journal*, 2(4):114–126, 1987.

112. B A Kitchenham. An evaluation of software structure metrics. In *Proceedings COMPSAC 88*, 1988.

113. B A Kitchenham. Empirical studies of assumptions that underlie software cost estimation models. *Information and Software Technology*, 34(4):211–218, 1992.

114. B A Kitchenham, L M Pickard and S J Linkman. An evaluation of some design metrics. *Software Engineering Journal*, 5(1):50–58, 1990.

115. B A Kitchenham and S J Linkman. Design metrics in practice. Technical report, Wolverhampton Polytechnic, 1990. Proceedings NDISD 89.

116. P Kokol. Using spreadsheet software to support metric life cycle activities. *SIGPLAN Notices*, 24(5):27–37, 1989.

117. A H Konstam and D E Wood. Software Science applied to APL. *IEEE Transactions on Software Engineering*, 11(10):994– 1000, 1985.

118. D H Krantz, R D Luce, P Suppes,and A Tversky. *Foundations of measurement*. Academic Press, 1971.

119. H E Kyburg. *Theory and Measurement*. Cambridge University Press, 1984.

120. I Lakatos. Falsification and the methodology of scientific research programs. In I Lakatos and A Musgrave, editors, *Criticism and the growth of knowledge*. Cambridge University Press, 1970.

121. J L Lassez, D J J van der Knijff, J Shepherd, and C Lassez. A critical examination of Software Science. *Journal of Systems and Software*, 2:105–112, 1981.

122. T Laurmaa and M Syrjanen. APL and Halstead's theory: a measuring tool and some experiments. *SIGMETRICS Performance Evaluation Review*, 1:32–47, Fall 1982.

123. R K Lind and K Vairavan. An experimental investigation of software

metrics and their relationship to software development effort. *IEEE Transactions on Software Engineering*, 15(5):649–653, 1989.

124. S Linkman and J Walker. Maintenance metrics (and how to avoid using them by controlling development programmes through measurement. *Information and Software Technology*, 1982.

125. B Liskov and J Guttag. *Abstraction and Specification in Program Development*. MIT Press, 1986.

126. A M Lister. Software Science — the emperor's new clothes? *Australian Computer Journal*, 14(2):66–71, 1982.

127. L T Love. An experimental investigation of the effect of program structure on program understanding. *SIGPLAN Notices*, 12(3):105–113, 1977.

128. L T Love and A B Bowman. An independent test of the theory of software physics. *SIGPLAN Notices*, 12(11):42–49, 1976.

129. G C Low and D R Jeffery. Function points in the estimation and evaluation of the software process. *IEEE Transactions on Software Engineering*, 16(1):64–71, 1990.

130. R D Luce. Semi-orders and a theory of utility discrimination. *Econometrica*, 24:178–191, 1956.

131. R D Luce and A A J Marley. Extensive measurement when concatenation is restricted and maximal elements may exist. In S Morgenbeser, P Suppes, and M G White, editors, *Philosophy, Science and Method: Essays in Honour of Ernest Nagel*. St. Martin's Press, 1969.

132. K Magel. Regular expressions in a program complexity metric. *SIGPLAN Notices*, 16(7):61–65, 1981.

133. T J McCabe. A complexity measure. *IEEE Transactions on Software Engineering*, 2(4):308–320, 1976.

134. T J McCabe. Structured testing: a testing methodology using the McCabe complexity metric. Technical report NB82NAAK5518l, National Bureau of Standards, 1982.

135. T J McCabe and C W Butler. Design complexity measurement and testing. *Communications of the ACM*, 32(12):1415–1425, 1989.

136. C L McClure. A model for program complexity analysis. In *Proceedings 3rd International Conference on Software Engineering*, pages 149–157, 1978.

137. A C Melton, D A Gustafson, J Bieman, and A Baker. A mathematical perspective for software measures research. *Software Engineering Journal*, 5(4):246–254, 1990.

138. R Milner. *Communication and Concurrency*. Prentice-Hall, 1989.

139. S N Mohanty. Software cost estimation: present and future. *Software Practice and Experience*, 11:103–121, 1981.

140. J C Munson and T M Khoshgoftaar. The relative software complexity metric: a validation study. In *Proceedings Software Engineering 90*,

1990.

141. J C Munson and T M Khoshgoftaar. The detection of fault-prone programs. *IEEE Transactions on Software Engineering*, 18(5):423–433, 1992.

142. G J Myers. *Reliable Software Through Composite Design*. Van Nostrand Rheinhold, 1975.

143. G J Myers. An extension to the the cyclomatic measure of program complexity. *SIGPLAN Notices*, 12(10):61–64, 1977.

144. P Naur and B Randell, editors. *Software Engineering: a Report on a Conference Sponsored by the NATO Science Committee*, 1969.

145. J K Navlakha. A survey of system complexity metrics. *Computer Journal*, 30(3):233–238, 1987.

146. R M Negrini and M Sami. Some properties derived from structural analysis of program graph models. *IEEE Transactions on Software Engineering*, 9(2):172–178, 1983.

147. K J Ottenstein. An algorithmic approach to the detection and prevention of plagiarism. *SIGCSE Bulletin*, 8(4):30–41, 1976.

148. L M Ottenstein. Quantitative estimates of debugging requirements. *IEEE Transactions on Software Engineering*, 5(5):504–514, 1979.

149. G Oulsnam. Cyclomatic numbers do not measure complexity of unstructured programs. *Information Processing Letters*, pages 207–211, December 1979.

150. E Oviedo. Control flow, data flow and program complexity. In *Proceedings COMPSAC 80*, pages 146–152, 1980.

151. M R Paige. A metric for software test planning. In *Proceedings COMPSAC 80*, pages 499–504, 1980.

152. D L Parnas. On the criteria to be used in decomposing systems into modules. *Communications of the ACM*, 15(2):1053–1058, 1972.

153. D L Parnas. Designing software for ease of extension and contraction. *IEEE Transactions on Software Engineering*, 5(2):128–138, 1979.

154. J Pfanzagl. *Theory of Measurement*. Physica-Verlag, 1968.

155. S L Pfleeger and C McGowan. Software metrics in the process maturity framework. *Journal of Systems and Software*, 12:255–261, 1990.

156. P Piowarski. A nesting level complexity measure. *SIGPLAN Notices*, 17(9):40–50, 1982.

157. D Potier, A R Ferreol, and A Bilodeau. Experiments with computer software complexity and reliability. In *Proceedings 6th International Conference on Software Engineering*, pages 94–103, 1981.

158. R E Prather. An axiomatic theory of software complexity metrics. *Computer Journal*, 27(4):42–45, 1984.

159. R E Prather. On hierarchical software metrics. *Software Engineering Journal*, 2(2):42–45, 1987.

160. R E Prather. Comparison and extension of theories of Zipf and Halstead. *Computer Journal*, 31(3):248–252, 1988.

161. R S Pressman. *Software engineering. A practitioner's approach.* McGraw-Hill, 1987.

162. D J Reifer. ASSET-R: A function point sizing tool for scientific and real-time systems. Technical Report RCI-TN-299, Reifer Consultants Inc., 1990.

163. R G Reynolds. Metrics to measure the complexity of partial programs. *Journal of Systems and Software*, 4(1):75–92, 1984.

164. H D Rombach. A controlled experiment on the impact of software structure on maintainability. *IEEE Transactions on Software Engineering*, 13(5):510–518, 1987.

165. H D Rombach and V R Basili. A quantitative assessment of software maintenance. In *Proceedings International Conference on Software Maintenance*, pages 134–144, 1987.

166. H D Rombach and B T Ulery. Improving software maintenance through measurement. *IEEE Proceedings*, 1989.

167. W B Samson, D G Nevill, and P I Dugard. Predictive software metrics based on a formal specification. *Information and Software Technology*, 29(5):242–248, 1987.

168. V Schneider. Approximations for the Halstead Software Science error rate and project estimators. *SIGPLAN Notices*, 23(1):40–47, 1988.

169. V Schneiderman and H M Hoffman. An experiment in software error data collection and analysis. *IEEE Transactions on Software Engineering*, 5(3):276–286, 1979.

170. N F Schneidewind. Methodology for validating software metrics. *IEEE Transactions on Software Engineering*, 18(5):410– 422, 1992.

171. R W Selby and V R Basili. Error localization during maintenance: generating hierarchical system descriptions from source code alone. In *Proceedings International Conference on Software Maintenance*, 1988.

172. V Y Shen. The relationship between student grades and software science parameters. In *Proceedings COMPSAC 79*, pages 783–787, 1979.

173. V Y Shen, S D Conte, and H E Dunsmore. Software Science revisited: a critical analysis of the theory and its empirical support. *IEEE Transactions on Software Engineering*, 9(2):155–165, 1983.

174. V Y Shen and H E Dunsmore. Analysing COBOL programs via Software Science. Technical report, Department of Computer Science, Purdue University, 1981.

175. V Y Shen, T J Yu, S Thebaut, and L Paulsen. Identifying error-prone software — an empirical study. *IEEE Transactions on Software Engineering*, 11(4):317–324, 1985.

176. M J Shepperd. A critique of cyclomatic complexity as a software metric. *Software Engineering Journal*, 3(2):317–324, 1988.

177. M J Shepperd. An empirical study of design measurement: an interim

report. Technical report 88/08, School of Computing and Information Technology, Wolverhampton Polytechnic, 1988.

178. M J Shepperd. An evaluation of software product metrics. *Information and Software Technology*, 30(3):177–188, 1988.

179. M J Shepperd and D C Ince. Design metrics and software maintainability: an experimental investigation. *Journal of Software Maintenance*, 3(4):215–232, 1991.

180. M J Shepperd. Early life cycle metrics and software quality models. *Information and Software Technology*, 32(4):311–316, 1989.

181. M J Shepperd. Measuring the structure and size of software designs. *Information and Software Technology*, 35(11):177–188, 1992.

182. M J Shepperd. An empirical study of design measurement. *Software Engineering Journal*, 5(1), 1990.

183. M J Shepperd. System Architecture Metrics: an Evaluation. PhD thesis, Open University, 1991.

184. M J Shepperd and D C Ince. Metrics, outlier analysis and the software design process. *Information and Software Technology*, 31(2):91–98, 1989.

185. M J Shepperd and D C Ince. Controlling software maintainability. In *Proceedings 2nd European Conference on Software Quality Assurance*, 1990.

186. M J Shepperd and D C Ince. The multi-dimensional modelling and measurement of software designs. In *Proceedings ACM Annual Conference*, 1990.

187. M J Shepperd and D C Ince. The use of metrics for the early detection of software design errors. In *Proceedings Software Engineering 90*, 1990.

188. P K Sinha, S Jayaprakash, and K B Lakshmanan. A new look at the control flow complexity of computer programs. In *Proceedings Software Engineering 86*, 1986.

189. C P Smith. A Software Science analysis of programming size. In *Proceedings ACM Annual conference*, pages 179–185, 1980.

190. I Sommerville. *Software engineering*. Addison-Wesley, 1992.

191. F Stetter. A measure of program complexity. *Computer Languages*, 9(3):203–210, 1984.

192. S S Stevens. On the theory of scales of measurement. *Science*, 103:677–680, 1946.

193. S S Stevens. Measurement, psychophysics and utility. In C W Churchman and P Ratoosh, editors, *Measurement: Definitions and Theories*. Wiley, 1959.

194. W P Stevens. *Structured Design*. Academic Press, 1980.

195. W P Stevens, G J Myers, and L L Constantine. Structured design. *IBM Systems Journal*, 13(2):115–139, 1974.

196. J M Stroud. The fine structure of psychological time. *Annals of the*

New York Academy of Sciences, pages 623– 631, 1966.

197. T Sunohara, A Takano, K Vehara, and T Ohkawa. Program complexity measure for software development management. In *Proceedings 5th International Conference on Software Engineering*, pages 100–106, 1981.

198. P Suppes. Measurement, empirical meaningfulness and three-valued logic. In C W Churchman and P Ratoosh, editors, *Measurement: definitions and theories*. Wiley, 1959.

199. P Suppes and J L Zinnes. Basic measurement theory. In B Lieberman, editor, *Contemporary Problems in Statistics*. Oxford University Press, 1971.

200. C R Symons. Function point analysis: difficulties and improvements. *IEEE Transactions on Software Engineering*, 14(1):2–11, 1988.

201. C R Symons. *Software Sizing and Estimating. Mk II FPA*. John Wiley, 1991.

202. P A Szulewski, M H Whitworth, P Buchan, and J DeWolf. The measurement of Software Science parameters in software designs. *SIGMETRICS Performance Evaluation Review*, pages 89– 94, Spring 1981.

203. R C Tausworthe. Deep space network software cost estimation model. Technical report 81-7, Jet Propulsion Laboratory, Pasadena, CA, 1981.

204. D A Troy and S H Zweben. Measuring the quality of structured designs. *Journal of Systems and Software*, 2(2):113–120, 1981.

205. W Turski and T Maibaum. *The Specification of Computer Programs*. Wiley–Interscience, 1985.

206. D J J van der Knijff. Software Physics and program analysis. *Australian Computer Journal*, 10:82–86, 1978.

207. A S Wang. The Estimation of Software Size and Effort: an Approach Based on the Evolution of Software Metrics. PhD thesis, Dept. of Computer Science, Purdue University, 1984.

208. A S Wang and H E Dunsmore. Back-to-front programming effort prediction. *Information Processing and Management*, 20(1–2):139–149, 1984.

209. E J Weyuker. Evaluating software complexity measures. *IEEE Transactions on Software Engineering*, 14(9):1357– 1365, 1988.

210. R W Whitty, N E Fenton, and A A Kaposi. A rigorous approach to structural analysis and metrication of software. *IEE Software and Microsystems*, 4(1):2–16, 1985.

211. R Wiener and R Sincovec. *Software engineering with Modula-2 and Ada*. Wiley, 1984.

212. N Wirth. *Systematic Programming, An Introduction*. Prentice-Hall, 1976.

213. S N Woodfield. Enhanced Effort Estimation by Extending Basic

Programming Models to Include Modularity Factors. PhD thesis, Department of Computer Science, Purdue Univ, 1980.

214. S N Woodfield, H E Dunsmore, and V Y Shen. The effect of modularisation and comments on program comprehension. In *Proceedings 5th International Conference on Software Engineering*, pages 215–223, 1981.

215. S N Woodfield, V Y Shen, and H E Dunsmore. A study of several metrics for programming effort. *Journal of Systems and Software*, 2:139–149, 1981.

216. M R Woodward, M A Hennell, and D A Hedley. A measure of control flow complexity in program text. *IEEE Transactions on Software Engineering*, 5(1):45–50, 1979.

217. S S Yau and J S Collofello. Some stability measures for software maintenance. *IEEE Transactions on Software Engineering*, 6(6):545–552, 1980.

218. S S Yau, J S Collofello, and T M MacGregor. Ripple effect analysis of software maintenance. In *Proceedings COMPSAC 78*, pages 60–65, 1978.

219. B H Yin and J W Winchester. The establishment and use of measures to evaluate the quality of software designs. In *Proceedings ACM Software Quality Assurance Workshop*, pages 45–52, 1978.

220. E Yourdon and L L Constantine. *Structured Design: Fundamentals of a Discipline of Computer Program and Systems Design*. Prentice-Hall, 1979.

221. J C Zolnowski and D B Simmons. Taking the measure of program complexity. In *Proceedings National Computer Conference*, pages 329– 336, 1981.

222. H Zuse. *Software Complexity. Measures and Methods*. de Gruyter, 1991.

223. H Zuse and P Bollmann. Software metrics: using measurement theory to describe the properties and scales of static complexity metrics. *SIGPLAN Notices*, 24(8):23–33, 1989.

224. S H Zweben and K Fung. Exploring Software Science relations in COBOL and APL. In *Proceedings COMPSAC 79*, pages 702–709, 1979.

INDEX